Praise

This book shares stories, in _____
friendships with Christian women has provided us strength, courage,
and hope as we raised our children, fought for our marriages, and built
our faith.

—Kay Robertson, from A&E _Duck Dynasty_

This book is packed with inspiration because it contains the secret for
connecting women's hearts to one another by establishing strong mentoring relationships. We all need friends who understand us and hold
us accountable. This is what Joneal Kirby has done through her Titus 2
ministry. She has tapped into hearts of all ages. As you read _Heartfelt_,
you will be challenged to enter into a victorious and biblical mandate
that will change your life, fulfilling God's purpose for you.

—Jane Graham, Samaritan's Purse

Heart to Home Ministry has been a big part of our church for over ten
years. Because of Joneal's vision to put Titus 2:3–5 into action, many
women have grown in their walk with God and in their roles as godly
wives and mothers. We have seen older and younger women fulfilling
the ancient model of spiritual mentoring. In _Heartfelt_, Joneal shows
how your home can be instrumental in building good relationships
and your family can grow to be all God wants it to be. This book is
a must-read for women wanting to impact others and build eternal
relationships.

—Al and Lisa Robertson,
from A&E _Duck Dynasty_, authors of _A New Season_

Heartfelt is equal parts manna and manual. In her warm and gracious
way, Dr. Joneal Kirby goes beyond explaining why women need to
build multigenerational relationships to nurture the body of Christ.
She shows us h~~

—Shellie _____ ll Things Southern"
of _Heart Wide Open_

Heartfelt is equal parts manna and manual. In her warm and gracious way, Dr. Joneal Kirby goes beyond explaining why women need to build multigenerational relationships to nurture the body of Christ. She shows us how.

—Shellie Rushing Tomlinson, "The Belle of All Things Southern"
and author of *Heart Wide Open*

There are times when a book inspires, motivates, and entertains. This is one of those times. *Heartfelt* will fill your heart with its messages of love from women who have shared their lives with each other. Thank you, Joneal, for giving thousands of women a voice. I couldn't be a prouder sister.

—Chrys Howard, author, *Duck Commander Devotions for Kids*
and *Miss Kay's Duck Commander Kitchen*

It's so refreshing to find a women's ministry that takes us back to the principles found in the New Testament church of the older women mentoring the younger women. Because we live in a world filled with hurts, hang-ups, and habits, women need support and encouragement and a resource for healthy, practical ways to help raise their families. I'm thankful Joneal commits her time to help women build strong, healthy families through the mentoring ministry Heart to Home. *Heartfelt* is filled with inspiring stories and will give you a blueprint in starting your own women's Titus 2 ministry.

—Mary Owen, National Celebrate Recovery Coach,
Saddleback Church, author of *Never Let Go*

In *Heartfelt*, Joneal shares her passion for living out Titus 2 and proven methods for connecting the godly wisdom of an experienced generation of mothers and grandmothers to younger women, both single and married, who long to honor God. On the world stage, people watch how Christian women do life—rearing children, maintaining marriages, sustaining careers. Joneal Kirby's work takes the phrase church family to a depth that God intended for His people. Implement this biblical practice, and the outcome will display a new joy and spiritual success—as Christian women lean on and learn from each other.

—Cathy Messecar, author of
A Still and Quiet Soul: Embracing Contentment

Wow! Joneal's heart for divorced women, single moms, remarried step-moms, and singles really shines through this book. I am so grateful for her authentic love for all women no matter what complexities have come their way. In *Heartfelt* I was able to peek into the real hearts of real women and it brought me to tears many times! All are loved and all matter to our loving God. Joneal's passion to reach all types of women is a beautiful reflection of the Heart to Home groups she hosts every week in her own home. I've seen it and it's real!

—Tammy Daughtry, MMFT
Founder, Co-parenting International and author,
Co-Parenting Works! Helping Children Thrive After Divorce

The work and ministry of Dr. Joneal Kirby has had a powerful, positive impact in my life. I've participated in her Heart to Home Ministry for two years, and this ministry has helped me grow and thrive in my home and in my spiritual life. Being a wife and working mother is challenging, and my mentoring group is a monthly oasis of love, friendship and sisterhood. *Heartfelt* captures the nurturing spirit of Heart to Home and I am confident that it will be a blessing to women all over the world. *Heartfelt* made me laugh and cry, and it especially helped me realize the importance of seeking love and relationships with other sisters in Christ. This book will make your day!

—Alex, daughter of Al and Lisa Robertson
of A&E *Duck Dynasty*

As someone who has been a Heart to Home fan since its very first year I was thrilled when I found out Joneal was writing this book. Heart to Home Ministry has changed my life in so many ways, and this book is sure to warm your heart and bring joy to your homes.

—Jil

In *Heartfelt*, Joneal guides women of God to live transparent lives not only before God but before each other. Only through transparency can we become a body that completely trusts and depends on one another. What a blessing and impact this book will have on so many lives! Joneal has touched my heart with her words. I truly look forward to sharing this message from God's Word with my sisters in my own church.

—Lee Ann

For the past ten years I have had the honor and pleasure of participating in Heart to Home Ministry with other women at my church. It has been a life-changing experience and has transformed the dynamics of my church family in a most positive way. In *Heartfelt*, Joneal nails it! She shows in the most vivid way how discipling, nurturing, and hospitality are the essence of meaningful connections in the church. It is a wonderful, quick read. I could not put it down! This book has all the key elements for building authentic relationships among God's women. And I know this because I have witnessed it in my life and in the lives of other women.

—Grace

Joneal is genuine and authentic, and so is her book! *Heartfelt* is a must-read—enlightenment for your heart and mind.

—Betty

I've been a part of the Heart to Home Ministry since it began, and it has had a significant impact on my life. I'm so thankful for Joneal's vision and her heart to guide and mentor me to be a stronger wife, mother, and friend! This book is truly heartfelt. It's a powerful tool to bring women spiritually together to a safe place, where they can be nurtured, mentored, and encouraged. Thank you, Joneal, for your heart and your passion for women.

—Debbie

Heart to Home Ministry is simply the best answer to helping Christian women connect in a large congregation. Paul knew Christian women needed this connection when he instructed Titus to encourage interaction between older and younger women in Titus 2. God's inspired Word gives us the simple answer to growing strong bonds among women, and Heart to Home is the best avenue by which this can be accomplished in today's busy world. Joneal Kirby has put together a simple and meaningful method by which Christian women can connect to one another through the Heart to Home Ministry, and I am thankful and grateful for all the work she has done in order to reach as many Christian women as possible.

—Gayle

heartfelt

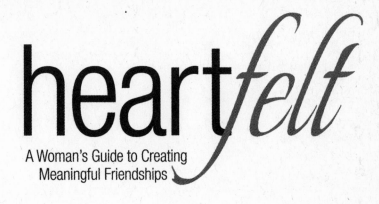

heart*felt*

A Woman's Guide to Creating
Meaningful Friendships

JONEAL KIRBY, PhD

WORTHY®
PUBLISHING

Published by Worthy Books, an imprint of Worthy Publishing Group, a division of Worthy Media, Inc., 134 Franklin Road, Suite 200, Brentwood, TN 37027.

WORTHY is a registered trademark of Worthy Media, Inc.
HELPING PEOPLE EXPERIENCE THE HEART OF GOD

eBook available wherever digital books are sold.

Library of Congress Cataloging-in-Publication Data

Kirby, Joneal.
   Heartfelt : a woman's guide to creating meaningful friendships / Joneal Kirby, PhD.
      pages cm
   Includes bibliographical references and index.
   ISBN 978-1-61795-422-1 (tradepaper : alk. paper)
   1. Christian women—Religious life. 2. Female friendship—Religious aspects—
Christianity. I. Title.
   BV4527.K478 2014
   248.8'43--dc23
                                             2014034475

Some names and identifying details have been changed to protect the privacy of the individuals involved.

For foreign and subsidiary rights, contact rights@worthypublishing.com.

ISBN: 978-1-61795-422-1

Cover Design: Stephanie D. Walker
Interior Design and Typesetting: Christopher D. Hudson & Associates, Inc.

Printed in the United States of America

15 16 17 18 19 VPI 8 7 6 5 4 3 2 1

To all the White's Ferry Road Church
Heart Moms, who believe in our
mentoring ministry so much that you give
unselfishly of your time and your talents,
your homes and your hearts, to make sure
we are obeying God's Word and making
disciples of God's women.

Contents

PART TWO

Making It Happen

OPEN HOMES

Experiencing the Fulfillment of Titus 2 Mentoring

> The glory of friendship is not the outstretched hand, nor the kindly smile, nor the joy of companionship. It is the spiritual inspiration that comes to one when [s]he discovers that someone else believes in [her], and is willing to trust [her] with [her] friendship.
> —*Ralph Waldo Emerson*

I have been a marriage therapist. A family counselor. An educator. A women's ministry leader. I am the oldest of six children, three of them girls. I am a wife, a mother, a daughter, a sister, a grandmother. I have hundreds of girlfriends, both close personal friends and Facebook friends. All that to say this: during my lifetime of teaching, counseling, speaking at conferences, leading small groups, and conversing with thousands of women, I have

learned a lot about women's emotional and spiritual needs.
We women have much in common, but one thing uniquely so:
we crave and seek out connection. We need relationships with
other women. And I mean authentic, meaningful, connecting
relationships, not just casual, everyday interactions. Friendship
with another Christian woman is a significant and beautiful and
necessary thing.

I know this firsthand. After getting married, my husband
and I moved closer to my parents and found jobs and an apart-
ment in the city where they were living. We were not just in a new
marriage but in a new town and in a new church, surrounded by
folks totally unfamiliar to us. It was a difficult, intimidating time
for me.

We joined the church where my parents were going. And
it was there that God did an amazing thing for me. I met some
of the friendliest, most warmhearted people I have ever known.
The congregation functioned as a small community of friendly,
wonderful people. They were a family, and they welcomed us
home.

The ladies of the congregation took me, a newbie wife, under
their nurturing wings and loved on me. I'm not ashamed to say
I was young and a rookie at anything to do with marriage and
building a home. I can recall those times now and laugh, but
back then ... I'm glad my husband stuck it out with me! I shouldn't
have worried, though. These amazing, loving ladies provided me
with recipes and household hints on everything from what laun-
dry soap to use to how to make great lasagna, from how to prepare to host company to how to clean up after they left. From
these women I learned how to practice hospitality, watching

them regularly open their homes and share their dinner tables. They had a dramatic and lasting impact on my life, especially Judy, Jan, Janet, Linda, Chris, and Karen, who were there for me during the early days of my marriage, during my pregnancies and the births of my three children, and beyond.

Those dozen-plus women who befriended me were wise and warm mentors. Most of them were only about ten years older than I was. A few of them were twenty or so years older. But they seemed so much more mature and experienced. I felt then, and still do today, that their attention to me and their genuine care of my family established my marriage and my early days of parenting on firm ground. These women's love of the Lord and His church were rock-solid examples that helped shape my growing faith and budding adult Christian life.

I want to be clear: it's not that I didn't cherish my own mother. My mom and I are very close. She has always been an amazing parent and wife—one of those rare, pioneer-spirit, courageous women who can do it all and do it all well. She gave me the firm foundation of a happy family life and a solid faith in God that I have never doubted. So I had my mother's heart and her ear whenever I needed it.

But having the additional voices of women friends from church was for me a blessing I had never imagined having—and now can't imagine not having. When my husband and I struggled with years of infertility, these friends were there to pray for us, hear my cries, and keep faith in God's plan for our family. When my children were finally born—in close succession—my church friends held baby showers for me, brought meals to us after each birth, invited our screamy-yelly family to Sunday dinners, and offered to babysit for the occasional date night. By helping with my babies, they made sure I could participate in Sunday school and church events and all the things I needed to keep my faith fed and healthy. And they helped me host my first home Bible study.

Most of what I learned from these women was taught through their influence and modeling. I learned about serving others from their example, not from their instruction. Sure, they sometimes sprinkled kind advice throughout our conversations, but never in a way that felt intrusive. I didn't resent or object to any of it. In fact, I was grateful they shared their sound counsel and godly wisdom with me.

One thing they did that has blessed me perhaps more than anything was encourage my love for speaking and teaching about Jesus and what our response to Him should look like. It was through their guiding, loving support that I became comfortable leading groups and teaching Bible classes. I can't begin to thank those women enough for the faith they had in me and the support they gave me, as my years with them were the beginnings of my ministry.

Fast-forward fifteen years or so. Our family moved to a smaller city and a much larger church. Again we moved having few friends and almost no familiarity with our new hometown. The church we joined was bigger, and the families there were well connected through longtime friendships and family relationships. Because of the close-knit community and size of the congregation, it took awhile to make close friends, but eventually we did. As my husband and I became involved with the ministries of the church, we began to teach family, marriage, and parenting classes. I was often with younger families, and in particular young wives and mothers.

About that time I noticed something: in this large church, as vibrant as it was, the younger women were not connecting with the older women as I had experienced in the smaller congregation where we had been. Where were the Jans and Judys and Karens I'd had in my life as a young married woman? Where were the intergenerational interactions I'd grown used to as I created a new life and family with my husband? I didn't really see those kinds of relationships in my new church. Yes, besides the younger women, there were many women my age in our church. And I had made some amazing friends among my peers. So I knew there was a wealth of wisdom and experience in the faithful women of my generation and beyond who could be a blessing to young wives and moms and the growing group of young single women.

Because I had developed close relationships with the younger women through parenting classes and my counseling work, I knew their desire to get to know well the other women in the church. And because I had been blessed to have wise, nurturing mentors as a young woman, I knew my experience could be duplicated. I wanted that more than anything—to help provide a way to bring these two amazing groups together.

During that time I had also been studying the instructions of Titus 2, a Bible passage with a distinct blueprint and instructions for godly mentoring. I knew the women in our church were not following that model. The more I read Titus 2 and the more I thought about it, I realized that passage was the key. We needed this kind of ministry between older women and younger women.

I became insistently passionate about the fact that we as women, as a church family, needed to be living out Titus 2 together. God was moving my heart to build a ministry—a women's ministry.

Ten years later I am thankful to say we made it happen—and very successfully. Our women's mentoring ministry has bridged the gap between generations and has built friendships between thousands of women in His church. These friendships are being used for mentoring, teaching, guiding, nurturing, supporting, and blessing His women. Women are forging deeply significant, spiritually meaningful relationships. And many lives are being changed—transformed—because of this intentional interaction.

I've noticed this about church life: many churchgoers are fine in the foyer. We're fine with the chitchat of "Hello" and "How are you?" This small talk is safe . . . and empty. It camouflages us. It's only when we get past what I call the foyer-facades that women can really connect and get to know one another. Only then are we able to share with one another our hurts, habits, and hang-ups, as well as our needs, desires, passions, and thanks.

I don't know about you, but my hurts, habits, and hang-ups don't go away when I enter the church building. I'd rather not carry them back out the door with me. But living a real life for Christ can be an almost daily challenge. What I need, and maybe what you need, is to have people in our lives who are there when we need a smile of encouragement, a shoulder to cry on, a prayer of petition, a blessing for support, and often a nudge to be better than we are.

What I am trying to get across to you, dear reader, is that life is hard enough with Christian friends. To try to do this life without them—well, that just seems impossible to me.

Let's take a look at the passage in Titus 2 that affected me so greatly.

> Likewise, teach the older women to be reverent in the way they live, not to be slanderers or addicted to much wine, but to teach what is good. Then they can urge the younger women to love their husbands and children, to be self-controlled and pure, to be busy at home, to be kind, and to be subject to their husbands, so that no one will malign the word of God. (vv. 3–5)

Now God gave many instructions for His people, His church, to follow. Most of them are not gender-specific. But there are a few gender-directed teachings in the Bible, and we women are mandated to follow those addressed to us. If we believe in God and believe His Word is the truth, then we must follow these passages. Titus 2:3–5 plainly states behaviors that God's women are to follow.

If we are to meant to follow the teachings of Titus 2, perhaps we need to delve into this passage a bit and see what we're getting into. Think of it like unpacking the boxes sent to us when we've ordered something large through the mail. When the item arrives, we have to assemble all those bits and pieces before we can use it. And the first, most important step is to make sure we have all the parts and understand the directions.

So let's unpack this passage of Scripture. First, we'll back up and look at verse 1 of the chapter. It says, "You, however, must teach what is appropriate to sound doctrine."

You must teach. Who must teach? Well, the apostle Paul is writing to Titus, who was the leader of the church, the pastor or elder. So everything that comes after that phrase, including the Titus 2 instructions written to women, is really a mandate to the entire church. The church and its leaders are being told to equip the entire congregation, including the women.

We need to understand how powerful this is. Women are to have an active, vital, ongoing relationship with the work of the local church. They are part of the total package of the ministry of the church. This means a Titus 2 ministry not only teaches and trains women but also encourages and builds up the entire congregation through its efforts to instruct and guide women in the way of the Lord.

The second thing we see in Titus 2:1 is that we are to "teach . . . sound doctrine." If I think of the word *sound* in relation to doctrine, as something that is whole or healthy, I think that we are to teach whatever is consistent or congruent with Scriptures. So whatever we teach in a women's ministry must be totally supported by the truth of the Bible. We aren't to teach our opinion or ideas from our educational training. The teachings of our ministry must be consistent with God's Word.

Another principle I see in this passage involves the relationships Paul is talking about. Through his words in Titus 2, he connects the fellowship of *all* the brothers and sisters in the congregation: older men, younger men, older women, younger women. Paul is describing an interactional connection between the members of the local church. To us, this command to connect with others means it's not just the leaders or the pastors or the evangelists who are to disciple the members. *We* are to disciple, teach, train one another. This is exactly what I experienced in the first church my husband and I were mentored in.

The point I'm making about these passages is that the women of the church are challenged in the same way the men are. Women's ministry is described here plainly. And I don't see this instruction as an option. It is a mandated behavior we are to follow in our local congregations.

Understand: none of the teaching, training, guiding, and befriending that is taught in Titus 2 can be done quickly or briefly. It will take time. It will require investing hours into one another to correctly "do" the work of discipling (teaching) women in our churches. Paul is describing a process of lives being invested into other lives—perhaps for many years, or even a lifetime.

In order to disciple as Jesus did, we must call each other "friends" (John 15:15). Being a friend gives us the relationship to influence one another, to impact each other's lives. Being friends with our church members means we are to know each other well. To rub our lives up against each other. To sharpen each other as stone against stone. To challenge each other. To encourage and to build up the faith and the spirits of each other. Jesus Himself modeled this discipling method of friend to friend through His group of twelve. I'd say His method is a good model for us to follow, don't you think?

What I have learned in my years in women's ministry is how to best facilitate the process. To be done well, women must meet regularly, routinely, and consistently in groups similar to the size of the discipling group Jesus managed. That is what a Titus 2 ministry does. It breaks down the congregation into smaller numbers so that we can get to know each other better and to teach one another well. We teach the older women to live reverent lives, worshipful and respectful of God's calling (Titus 2:3). And as they then teach the younger women to love their husbands and their children, to be pure and kind (vv. 4–5), they mirror the gospel of Jesus Christ to one another—and ultimately to the world, which includes our local communities as well as the mission fields.

As we build up the body of Christ, we will be better equipped to be salt and light in the unsavory and dark culture we live in (Matthew 5:13–16). We, as Titus 2 women, will model to people seeking to live a way that makes more sense. The result is that by being bodybuilders—building up the body of Christ— we strengthen the entire body of Christ, replacing our flawed human character with the character of Christ.

Finally, take a look at the last part of Titus 2:5. It tells us that if we women live as we are called to live, then we will not "malign"—or dishonor—the Word of God. Isn't that amazing? As we become more like God intends us to be as His women, we actually give honor to God's Word. Wow! That's a pretty good grade to receive for this test of biblical womanhood.

This will cost us, though. Sharing our lives with other women isn't easy. It means we must be open. We have to be tolerant. And patient. And forgiving. We have to drop our judgmental attitudes and opinions. We can't be close to someone we criticize. People won't trust us if we are gossiping about them. Women won't want to be our friends if we aren't friendly people.

And younger women who wish to learn from and be guided by older women will have to give up some of their time. And perhaps some of their activities and even some of the folks they may hang around with.

Can you imagine what would change in your church if a Titus 2 ministry were active there? Can you think with me for a moment what would be different as a result of women helping, guiding, teaching, and training other women to love God more, to love their husbands and their children more, to treat others with kindness and respect, to know God's Word better? And to do all this while becoming best friends, close confidants, trusted advisers to one another? Would anything be different in your church if this were going on?

From what I've explained, you can see how a Titus 2 women's mentoring ministry works: older women in the church befriending younger women. Sounds pretty basic. And it is, in principle. In practical terms, though, it may not be so simple. But there is a model that works. I've experienced it. Many women have. And that's what this book is about. Since a Titus 2–based women's mentoring ministry is a bit more complicated to explain than it is to actually do, I've shared a few stories that best model it. When you read about these women's lives, you will see the Titus 2 model come to life. You will see how I developed real, authentic relationships with godly women who have helped me grow and mature as I strive to become the best Christ-servant I can be. You will also hear the voices of many others who have done the same, who have approached relationship building—perhaps doubtful and hurting, perhaps longing and trusting—with the goal of mentoring. Not only that, through a Titus 2 ministry they have found true, deep friendships. You will learn how they made connections in their churches with women at similar stages in life and with older, wiser women. And how those relationships changed them.

Finally, you will have a blueprint for your own Titus 2 possibilities, including a snapshot of Heart to Home, the Titus 2–based mentoring ministry I created.

Since you may know some people in your church, you may have friends—good Christian women—who are spiritual leaders, trusted advisers, a support team, and happy spirits. All of them can join with you on your journey toward Titus 2. I pray that those friendships deepen and become richer and more intentionally spiritual. I also pray that you are able to create a support system that will enrich and nourish your life for years to come.

My prayer for you is truly heartfelt: if you don't already have those friendships in your life, I pray that after reading this book you will know how to find them. I promise it will be an amazing experience.

God bless you.

PART ONE

Finding What You're Looking For

What is home? My favorite definition is "a safe place," a place where one is free from attack, a place where one experiences secure relationships and affirmation. It's a place where people share and understand each other. Its relationships are nurturing. The people in it do not need to be perfect; instead, they need to be honest, loving, supportive, recognizing a common humanity that makes all of us vulnerable.

—*Gladys Hunt*

CHAPTER ONE

OPEN TO OTHERS

A Vulnerable Heart
Is an Authentic Heart

> I spent a lot of years trying to outrun or
> outsmart vulnerability by making things
> certain and definite, black and white,
> good and bad. My inability to lean into
> the discomfort of vulnerability limited the
> fullness of those important experiences
> that are wrought with uncertainty: love,
> belonging, trust, joy, and creativity, to
> name a few.
>
> —*Brené Brown*

MARANDA'S STORY

I ended up in my Titus 2 group in a roundabout way. I
didn't grow up with a church background at all. So I didn't
have mentoring on my radar. I didn't even have God on
my radar. And my life was suffering from it. I was suffering. I had reached the point where I was out of control
and my marriage was about to fall apart.

As a last-ditch effort, my husband and I started going to counseling. Actually, he went first, before I ever thought of going. He was desperate for help. "I'm just going to bring her to you and you need to help her," he told the counseling staff. "I don't know what that will look like, but I trust you all will know." He turned me over into their hands. That may sound presumptuous to some people—to think he more or less said I needed fixing—but he was right. And I'm so grateful that he loved me enough to take that first step.

Through our counseling I was introduced to church. When I started attending I didn't know a soul—there were about eight hundred people who worshipped there, and it was overwhelming to me. Besides that, I felt self-conscious about my lack of church background. Everyone knew their Bible, talked about their faith, lived and breathed their relationship with God. I had none of that. And with my insecurities, I didn't feel comfortable making personal connections. So I sat there alone in a sea of people. It wasn't their fault. I simply wasn't ready or able to open up to them.

To help, someone suggested I try the church's Titus 2 women's mentoring ministry. I was skeptical about how they thought that could make a difference when I wasn't open to interacting with people in general. But in the end I agreed to go. I was at the point where I knew I needed to change things in my life—change things in me—but I didn't know what to do or how to make it happen. *Okay,* I thought. *Maybe this will help.*

So I went to the women's gathering I'd heard so many people talking about. I didn't know much about it other than that it was geared toward women. I also pretty much didn't know anyone there that night, but everyone was very welcoming and kind. Coming from my background, that was incredible. I'd been absolutely certain no one would accept me. I had so much baggage. I figured they'd be polite but pretty much leave me alone.

I couldn't have been more wrong. They welcomed me with open arms and treated me just like all the other girls there. We had supper and chatted, then we gathered for Bible study and talk. I couldn't really contribute much to the discussion, but I sat there taking it all in, watching and listening to these women. It seemed a relatively painless experience—definitely better than I expected it to be.

That night, however, something out of the ordinary happened: one of the mentors confessed that she didn't know why, but she felt led by the Holy Spirit to reveal her personal story. So everyone quieted down and she began to talk. It was not a pretty story, but she didn't shy away from relating all the painful and dirty details. She'd never shared them before, at least to that group, so it was new to everyone there, and I'm sure her story surprised a lot of people.

I know it surprised me. Her story absolutely floored me. It felt like every word she said related directly to me, that every experience she'd had was mine. I couldn't believe it—I'd kept my own experiences hidden away in shame and fear, trying to disguise and ignore them. And yet here she was, opening herself up to the group and allowing herself to be vulnerable and exposed so she could minister to us younger women. It was an incredible moment, one I know God had engineered in both her life and mine.

Well, afterward I was in a fog. But I mostly held myself together until the meeting was over and I got to the car. I climbed in, set my things down, and then I proceeded to fall apart. I sat there by myself and sobbed . . . in relief. You see, I couldn't believe there were people in the church like me—women who had suffered and had been emotionally broken down until they didn't know what to do. I didn't know that even godly, churchgoing women had lives that were not only imperfect but sometimes even painful and ugly. I simply hadn't accepted that possibility before. All I'd ever seen in church were happy people who seemed to have their lives all together.

But that night I realized I'd been completely wrong. These women's lives were not perfect. It was what they did with those lives and how they overcame their problems that mattered. I realized, *It's okay to be a mess! I just have to believe things are going to start changing.*

From that point on, I was hooked on Titus 2 mentoring. I remember a friend telling me, "Go in there and let them love on you and care about you. Trust me: they will." And they did. And I ran with it. I clung to whomever I could get my hands on, asked every question I could, went to every meeting I could. Sometimes I even went to two different Titus 2 groups' meetings. I wanted it all!

And every mentor I came into contact with became my mom. That's what the relationships I've gained are—these women are truly moms to me and I call them that. I didn't have a good background as far as parents. I had a mom and she loved me. But our relationship was based on friendship, nothing more. We'd never had a true mother-daughter relationship. It wasn't until I experienced the connections I made with my Titus 2 mentors that I finally realized—or admitted to myself—I needed a real mom. I'd needed one all along.

Well, with these women, I found not just one, not just two, but many moms. And even more sisters. I suddenly had the type of family I'd always longed for. Each year there were new ladies to get to know, and each year I grew close to all of them. And I continue to grow closer to these women. Even though a particular group may break apart at the end of the year and we go our separate ways, I know without a doubt those women are still going to be there for me, giving me opportunities to be real, to be vulnerable, to be authentic. They're there for me in good times and when I have troubles. And I'll be there for them too. I'll have those friendships forever. Every true relationship I've ever had started at my Titus 2 ministry.

My time with these small groups has blessed me in ways I can't even describe. Growing up, I had major trust issues. None of my relationships had lasted. The other person always quit on me or told me how horrible I was. So my self-esteem when I walked into the Titus 2 women's gathering that first night was lower than the floor. I didn't think I was worth anything, and I definitely didn't think I could have a relationship with anyone. I couldn't even make my own family want to have anything to do with me. And my marriage was having troubles because of my emotional and spiritual issues.

But my mentoring family took me in. They told me, "We're not going to leave you. We're here for you. We love you. And we're going to help you through your trials. Don't think that every time something bad happens or every time we may not agree on things or every time we try to help you with something you're not comfortable with we're going to walk out on you. We will not abandon you. Those days are over."

And they have not abandoned me. Instead, these women taught me how to be a strong woman of God when I never thought I could be, because I had always felt I wasn't good enough. They taught me that when your world is cracked, you can pick up the pieces and put it back together again. They taught me how to be a wife when I didn't know how because I'd never seen it modeled. And they taught me how to be a mom—how to be loving and caring and forgiving and a leader in my children's own paths toward God.

My Titus 2 women have always been real with me too. If there is something they feel I need to hear or do—as a mom, wife, or woman—they take me under their wings and teach me. Show me. They don't always pat me on the back and tell me what I want to hear. For instance, when my husband and I were having problems, I had a lot of outside people wanting to give me advice on how to do things—advice that often revolved around "Do what's best for yourself." But my mentors told me I had to do what was best for our *marriage*. They modeled what a real relationship was and challenged me to live the same way, to forgive and to grow. They gave me the advice I needed, not what I wanted to hear. And it has made all the difference in my life. I'm blessed to say my marriage and family are happy and whole.

Of course not all of it was easy. A lot of it was very hard. I've had moments when I thought—and sometimes still do—*I'm never going to make it to the place they want for me or be the person they think I am.* I've had moments when I looked at myself and was positive I didn't have it in me to succeed. But that's because I was focusing on the wrong things. I was focusing on my insecurities. I thought I had to look a certain way, to act a certain way, to be somebody completely different from myself, because I was never accepted the way I was. I thought it was all about the exterior, because that's what was instilled in me.

Through my mentoring relationships, I've learned that it truly isn't the exterior but the interior that matters. So that's what I've worked on. Because what's on the inside is going to be reflected on the outside. My heart and soul are more important than anything else could ever be. That's all that matters.

That's been the hardest thing for me to learn, but in the past few years I've changed a lot. It's been rough, but with the help of my mentors I've worked on it. I had to learn to open up and be vulnerable—because I wasn't, not by a long shot. I had to understand that no matter how much I messed up, no matter how much I struggled and worried, I could reveal it all and acknowledge it and move on because God loved me.

It's taken a long time to get to that place. In the beginning I could say God loved me, but I didn't really believe it. I thought, *How could He love me? Nobody loves me*. But I've learned to accept love and accept myself even when it's not comfortable. God *does* love me.

I told my husband the other day, "You know, I like myself. I *like* myself." Most people wouldn't think anything of that statement. But most people don't realize what a hard thing—an impossible thing—that once was for me to say. My Titus 2 family does. They know where I came from and the journey that brought me to those words. And these women are a huge part of how I got to this point. I am not the girl who walked through the door that night so long ago. I've come so far since then that I don't know who she was. And I certainly don't ever want to see her again. I'm pretty sure I never will.

No, I *know* I never will.

Maranda's story may or may not be one you've seen before. It was not an easy one to live, she will tell you. What's amazing about her experience, though, is the absolute transformation a Titus 2 ministry had in her life. Ten years ago she was in no way the kind of person who'd be interviewed for a book. She was a mess—hurting, miserable, painfully insecure, boxed in. And she couldn't see her way out of it. She had withdrawn, physically and emotionally, from her life and her marriage. Her body curved in on itself, and she kept her head down and spoke softly and hesitantly. She was like a shadow.

That's no longer the case. Now Maranda is a confident woman, led by the Holy Spirit and a strong ambassador for women's small group ministries. She is a wise and loving mother and wife. She has the courage to speak out about herself and her struggles, where she was and where she's come to. She is transformed.

Why? Because she was open to learning from other women and becoming who God wanted her to be. And that was a crucial element. It's all about the attitude. If you cannot find a way to open yourself to others and let them in, you are bound to fail. It is simply impossible to be helped if you're closed up and hiding your hurts and struggles. Not Maranda, though. Once she realized her need, she tore open the doors to her heart. She allowed others in and she actively sought their guidance, presenting to them a teachable spirit. She fought for her life, for her marriage, for her family. And the Holy Spirit blessed her through providing loving mentoring relationships.

That's the ultimate goal of this book, dear reader: for you to understand what it means to be vulnerable and relational, so the wise women in your life can reach into your heart and help you.

Maranda agrees. "I've learned that no matter how broken you are—and I've been to the point where I thought there was no hope for me—if you give yourself to a mentoring relationship with open arms and open heart and open eyes and without any expectation other than letting your mentor love you, you will be blessed. No matter where you are, God gives you these women,

Because it's guaranteed at least some of them will have experience with the same things you've been uncertain about sharing. And I promise you that once one of you begins to open up, it's usually the trigger that opens a floodgate of similar responses. Everyone is rushing to add her own experiences, to validate what another has said, to offer encouragement. In that way vulnerability brings strength as you all begin to lean on and support each other without fear of any negative backlash.

I cannot understate how liberating that is.

So, my friend, I leave you with this: if you can remember that none of us is perfect, that we all have fears and hurdles (and hopes and dreams), but we're all moving in the same direction—toward God—then you've already taken the first step. Maranda did, and look where her journey took her. If she had not made that choice to open up, though, I honestly do not know where she would be today.

In the chapters to come, we will look at different ways in which a Titus 2 mentoring ministry can enrich you. By the time we're done, my hope is that you will be ready and willing to make something similar happen in your own life. Take the next step! You won't be disappointed.

Heart Check

Two are better than one,
    because they have a good return for their labor:
If either of them falls down,
    one can help the other up.
But pity anyone who falls
    and has no one to help them up.
                                —Ecclesiastes 4:9-10

Have you found yourself hiding behind safe responses and arm's-length conversations, even at church or with friends? If so, how has that worked out for you?

_____

_____

_____

_____

What would it mean to you to enter into a Titus 2 relationship with other women where anything goes and you have the freedom to show your true self and life?

_____

_____

_____

_____

Do you know someone else who needs to feel the freedom of vulnerability? Would you be willing to approach her? Why?

_____

_____

_____

_____

God, give me the strength to be open to others even when I'm reluctant and to understand that by doing so I am allowing You access to me. You know the godly women I need in my life and those who will accept me in my vulnerability. Guide me to them.

Women thrive on relationships. We need them. We want them. So it was limiting and frustrating—at least to me—to be part of a body of believers that did not have a way to draw younger and older women together. As a thirty-two-year-old woman, I yearned for a way to get to know and build relationships with mature believers. My friends and I knew that our church was full of deeply rooted, godly women. We knew they had things to teach us and things we could learn from them. We wanted to get to know them. We just didn't know how to meet them. And truthfully, although we were desperate to connect with them, we weren't sure they wanted to meet or know us.

It has therefore been a blessing to finally have a Titus 2 ministry that bridges the gap between the generations! We are finally getting to sit at the feet of these older Christian women and listen to them. And we know that despite our age differences, we're still the same. So many times I've heard a mentor say, "I've been there" or, "One thing that I've learned that's so important is . . ." or even, "If there's one thing I regret, it's spending so much time worrying about . . ." That alone has been a rewarding experience.

And we are able to learn from all the experiences of these mature believers. Just like Titus 2 says, we *need* these women to show us how to be good moms and wives, how to be hospitable. We need their encouragement to build us up and mentor us. The world puts so much pressure on us, and we need to be shepherded and discipled by strong women of God who can help us combat these worldly, unfounded pressures and help us stay focused on what is truly important.

Not only that, but as a body of believers it is integral for us as women to know each other well. It's important for us not to put on pretensions in front of one another and worry about how our house isn't picked up or how we don't have on any makeup, but instead to be real with one another. I've learned that I'll survive, and I now have a few friends I can just be myself around—no judgment at all. No makeup, a dirty house, misbehaving kids . . . no problem! They will take me as I am. They'd rather put their focus on *me* than on my belongings or appearance.

They care about the prayer requests I'm afraid sound silly to the rest of the world. They love me through my bad moods. They love me through dry spells when my faith is waning, when I feel like I'm out of prayers and out of energy. Through all of this, these ladies never judge, always listen, and shower me with an abundance of encouragement and grace.

I would love for all women to get to experience the support of a Titus 2 small group. Relationships like these are so important to a church body! Every woman needs a lot of Christian women like this in their lives. I think we'd all be in a better place—a place of strength—if we had more opportunities to unconditionally love and share with each other.

—AMANDA, MENTEE

My experience with a Titus 2 ministry has been filled with real joy at opening my home to our group. I have other friends who serve as mentors as well, stepping up to the plate and opening their homes too. It's been a rewarding experience for all of us. We came together as one unit to serve our young ladies. More important, we specifically set out to glean from the younger ones where they were in their spiritual walk within their families and church and what they needed from us. And then we worked to make sure we provided that for them.

We set forth at the beginning to make this a fun journey for all of us, yet there were times when we discovered difficult situations the girls sometimes experienced. This only served to make us more attentive to our relationships and our support, especially in prayer. We understood the need to honor the girls' honesty and vulnerability with our responses and our commitment to them. And to foster commitment among the girls as well.

Because of everyone's openness, the relationships that developed during our few hours together each month became priceless! This time knit our personalities together and formed a bond that never could have developed by just seeing one another at church or being involved in an activity at the church building. It was the intimacy in our small groups that cultured the relationships. The older women learned the different personalities of the younger ones and were better able to minister to them on an individual basis. The younger women became more open to the older women and grew to respect our years of experience.

And may I say, we older women have learned as much from the younger! We didn't expect that, but we all quickly learned they had things they could teach us as well.

I believe a Titus 2 ministry gives us all a renewed sense of purpose in mentoring women. We trust that God will lead us in each meeting, and we desire the treasured blessings He grants us each time we meet. We enjoy our meal together around the table, and the good conversations and prayer time makes all of us look forward to the next meeting. In fact, when the season ends, no one wants the group to break up. But we've discovered how wise it is to say our good-byes and then to re-form into new groups so that we can develop more as godly women and can create new relationships while still savoring the past ones, which never go away. The process is about maturing and growing in the Lord, and it has everything to do with being open to fellowship.

It's been a wonderful journey, and I know we've all been blessed by it, both the young and the older. We've seen each other's hearts and are the better for it.

—GEORGETTE, MENTOR

CHAPTER TWO

OPEN HEARTS

Never Alone

Women have strengths that amaze men.
They bear hardships and they carry burdens,
but they hold happiness, love and joy. . . .
They'll drive, fly, walk, run or e-mail you,
to show how much they care about you.
The heart of a woman is what makes the world
   keep turning.
They bring joy, hope, and love.
They have compassion and ideas.
They give moral support to their family and friends.
Women have vital things to say and
   everything to give.
                      —Unknown

MISSY'S STORY

My life is typical of many modern moms. Go, go, go, go . . . a never-ending montage of places to be and people to talk to and family to take care of. Because of that, it's sometimes a struggle to find time for myself—and for fellowship on a meaningful level. I know a lot of other women in the same situation. When we get together, we're talking about our kids and how they scored in the big game or discussing jobs or our husband's latest adventure. Maybe we're even trying to one-up each other a bit, although we'd never admit that, even to ourselves. What we're not doing is getting to the heart of what Jesus said about true fellowship.

We need to challenge women to get deeper into each other's lives, to get beyond the casual pre-church or supermarket-aisle conversations. More important, we need to intentionally support each other in the midst of all the craziness we all experience on a day-to-day basis.

My Titus 2 group has done exactly that for me. I, like so many other women, have had a healthy supply of ups and downs in my life. Some have been relatively minor and some have been very significant. Painful, even. I can honestly say my women's mentoring groups—their loving support and the advice they gave through the years— are what got me through each and every one of them. Too many times to count I've said, "Help! I don't know what I'm doing!" or, "I'm overwhelmed" or, "I honestly don't think I can get through this." And they've given me answers and prayer. That's how I relate the past years— in terms of the challenges I've had and how the different groups I was a part of got me through them. Or at least helped me endure them.

One of the benefits of the support I receive from these women is its immediacy. Sometimes I'm able to ask for advice during a meeting and get some responses right away. Sometimes it's a text or phone call that's returned almost as soon as I send or make it. Whatever the case, these women are there for me. I've had help with home life and behavioral issues with the kids. I've had help with mentoring on a personal goal and things I need to do to improve my life and my relationships. I've had help by simply gaining strength from the women in my group during those moments of "What do I do when I get home? How do I make it through tonight?" We've all had those nights, right? We've all had those needs.

And those challenges really bring us together as a group. Women gravitate toward social settings. We seek connections. God hardwired us that way when He put us in charge of families. So that's not a hard thing. What's difficult is feeling that you're in a place where you can be vulnerable. That you have absolute confidentiality and the protection of a group that has your back no matter what. You get that with a Titus 2 ministry. You understand that whatever is revealed there stays there. We share some pretty heartfelt things, some things that for whatever reason we'd rather not put out there in the mainstream. And we're confident we can do so.

Sharing your own challenges also means others feel confident to do the same. And next thing you know, you're all contributing and confirming and exploring your similar experiences. And you gain perspective as you realize everyone has her own struggles to overcome. Maybe not that day or week or month. But we've all got them. What a gift it is to be able to unburden ourselves.

You may think, *Okay, but your mentoring group only meets a few hours a month. How in the world could you become so close to those women that you feel comfortable sharing everything? Is it really like that?*

It really is. You really do share everything. Opening up to each other creates an intimacy that truly connects you. The more you share, the stronger the connection, until you reach the point where you honestly don't even hesitate to let your heart out. You're confident that these women get you. They've heard you all season long; they know the backstories.

And there are so many women! With our particular ministry, we go into different groups each year. So each year the dynamic is slightly different because each set of mentors is different and each set of sisters is different. Each group is unique and wonderful. And I've made some incredible friendships because of them. Yes, it might take a little time to loosen up to each other at the start of the year. But most of the women have been sharing their lives in other groups, so even though we may be new to each other at the beginning, we understand the need for vulnerability and confidentiality. So we just go for it. That's so freeing!

One thing I especially love about our small group meetings is the sense of servanthood from our mentors. They've been where we younger women are. They remember how it felt, how sometimes you're mired in the moment and can't see beyond the next task on the list. They know what it feels like to be tired or cranky from a nonstop week. They understand how hard it is to step away from the hubbub and responsibility and just breathe. So their mission for the night is to pamper us. That was something that really took time for me to get used to, especially the first year. I had a leader who was such a giver. And my personality is a doer. At the time I had an eight-year-old, a five-year-old, and a newborn, so I was constantly in high gear. I'd get up in the morning and go full tilt and never even think of myself all day long. A typical modern woman.

To go to group night and suddenly be expected to turn that off was almost impossible. But that's what we were expected to do. Required to do! The whole evening was about the older women serving us younger women. We'd come in and our mentors would have a hot or cold drink for us, depending on the season. Then they'd sit us down and bring us dinner—actually plate the food for us! And afterward they would not let us help clear up anything. They'd say, "No, no, no! Sit! Enjoy yourselves."

The doer in me found that incredibly difficult to obey. I thought I should be helping, like anyone would naturally do with a hostess. All us younger ones did, really. But the mentors insisted.

As the year progressed I slowly began to relax and enjoy that night—being able to go over there and unwind and accept that the leaders wanted to take care of us younger ladies, wanted to minister to us. It wasn't even a chore for them. It wasn't like they were thinking, *Ugh, when everybody leaves we have to do the dishes and clean up.* No, they couldn't wait for us to get there so they could treat us. It was an amazing experience for all of us tired young women.

Another thing I loved was how everything was planned out by the mentors. They always had a set routine for the night and had prearranged everything for us. Now, I've spent years leading groups in my own home, so I knew there was a lot of responsibility involved regarding what you want to accomplish in a night—what to say, what to study, how to facilitate and lead conversations. At first I was like, *Okay, do I need to get in here and help out?* And then I realized, *No, I don't. I can talk if I want to, I can lean back and listen if I want to. I can contribute however much I want. That's all!* It was liberating. I felt like my needs were being taken care of and I didn't have to fulfill someone else's.

It's funny. Before I actually joined that first group, when I thought about the Titus 2 verses and about older women training younger ones, I always pictured a class setting, like a parenting class. Like, "Okay, ladies, now we're going to teach you this . . ." I never really thought about it as anything more. But as I began to under-stand everything my group offered me, I realized it was much more fulfilling and rewarding than just a class. Much richer in experience, especially in terms of relation-ships and support. And I came to see it as a necessity for my life.

Even still, I needed to make it a priority. Why is it that the times we need fellowship the most are the times it's hardest to make happen? Our lives pull at us, in big and small ways, until we find ourselves without the support we need. That's when we must be the most intentional about making it happen. That scheduled time of getting together for a few hours each month—it's something we have to require in our schedule. It can't be optional.

With my small group, I had to get into my head that it was okay to make time for it. It was okay to drop every-thing at home and know the world wouldn't fall apart if I disappeared for a few hours. I'll admit that was hard, because often it meant I had to adjust my expectations of what would happen while I was gone. At first I thought, *All right, I'm doing something good. I'm helping my mar-riage, helping the relationship by learning from these women how to be a better wife, a better mom. This is great. I can do this.*

In return I figured my husband, Jase, would have the dishes done, the house tidied, the kids taken care of, and be ready to welcome me home and hear about the insights I'd gained that night. I pictured us cozying up on the couch when I got home from our small group meet-ing while I excitedly shared all we'd learned.

Yeah, didn't happen. It didn't matter what time I came home, the supper I'd cooked was still sitting out, the kids were asleep on the floor, toys and things everywhere . . . I'd be like, "Really?" And *boom,* the good vibe would be gone. I'd have this attitude of *grumble, grumble, grumble*, stomping around putting away the food, picking everything up, packing the kids off to bed. And Jase would shake his head and say, "I don't know about this mentoring thing. You always come home in a bad mood."

So for a while I'd go to the meetings and sit there thinking, *Okay, when I get home it's gonna be bad. I've got to accept that fact, work on my attitude. This is still worth it.* But I'd tell the other ladies, "You've got to pray for me!"

Then I realized something: there were a lot of other moms in the group going through the same thing, having that same stressed-out feeling about all the housework and family needs they knew were waiting at home for them. They were nodding their heads and saying, "Yes! It's like that at my house too!" And strange as it sounds, that revelation was so freeing. Just knowing we were all in the same boat helped us sit back, take a breath, and realize, "Hey, it's okay."

And it reinforced in us the need to take that time for ourselves, no matter what. Because otherwise we'd never stop.

We have to be intentional about "our time." The group meeting has to go on the calendar, and we have to know nothing's going to move it off. Then we look forward to it, to getting away from the chaos, the kids' homework, and baths. (And let's be real: they probably won't have baths that night. But that's not the end of the world.)

In the end I think the most important part of a mentoring group is the authenticity of being there for each other. We provide something we all desperately need in our lives: unconditional support. I've experienced it for so long now I don't even know what I would do without it. Honestly, I don't want to think about it. But I can think of others who don't have what I have, what the others in our group have. I've had women tell me so. Yes, they're in churches. But they're still not fulfilled, not making meaningful connections. They're trying to lead a spiritual life in isolation, and they're longing for something more. I tell them, "Small groups. Get out of the big church auditorium, where people don't really know you, and get into your homes. You may not have a dozen women or even six, but you can at least have a couple of you together, intentionally supporting each other."

Women need women. Period. We need to bring each other into our personal spaces and lives and learn—or relearn—how to lean on each other. We have to make it happen. The rewards are too huge not to. The results are too important not to.

Missy has always been immersed in fellowship. She has a great mother—a wonderful woman. She's had godly friends. She attends an active church. But those things haven't necessarily meant that Missy had mentors. Mentoring encompasses a whole separate element of our faith journey. And there's something distinctly different and fulfilling in what you receive from a Titus 2 mentoring situation; there's value in being intentionally placed with a group of peers where you can build relationships under the guidance of a mentor. Paul writes, "Strive for full restoration, encourage one another, be of one mind, live in peace. And the God of love and peace will be with you" (2 Corinthians 13:11). But how often are we intentional about gathering together not just for Bible study but to support and encourage each other?

Not nearly often enough. Which is sad, because when women are completely committed to fellowship, lives are blessed.

When they're not committed? Well, it's no secret that families are disintegrating around us. Lives are falling apart because women have no support network. They don't know where to go when they have a need or a crisis or when they have victories to celebrate. They're soldiering on alone, which means no one knows when to reach out to them. We don't know each other well enough to even feel any need to reach out. Instead, we see unhappiness and too many marriages falling apart because we're so disconnected that others can't see something's going on and step in to say, "Let me help you. Let me pray for you." It's affecting us generationally as well, as our children suffer the consequences.

One of the most important aspects of a Titus 2 ministry is learning how to connect in authentic relationships with one another. We've got to get godly women to become real with each other, and small groups are the only way to do it. Church services are not the place for this type of relationship. It's not that church isn't important. It is—vitally so. But it serves a different purpose. Small groups serve another.

And it's not that women don't want small group connections. But we have to lead them to it, almost force them into a situation where they begin to experience it, begin to feel safe. When you get them to that place, it's then easy for the Holy Spirit to take over and restore them. Trust me, that does and will happen, every time. And when it does, it transforms lives. Women are uplifted. Blessed. Nurtured. Educated. They are made whole.

Most important, they learn they have resources that will never go away. There is always someone there, someone to talk to or learn from or pray with.

One of the things I specifically foster in my own women's mentoring ministry is the younger women seeing their mentors as surrogate mothers. Moms love unconditionally. They take their kids where they are. They hang in there with them. They may have to discipline, but they do it with love. Likewise, the mentors take seriously their responsibility toward the younger women in their groups. They meet them where they are. The mentors can look back at how they themselves were at certain ages. Sometimes they can relate to the younger women's situations, sometimes not. Occasionally they, too, must step out in faith and take a younger woman to task for unwise decisions and lifestyles. But no matter what, they love unconditionally.

So there's a part of Titus 2 mentoring that requires an atmosphere of flexibility and caring, and mentors teach that to the younger generation. Mentor groups remind us to drop our critical nature, become more tolerant and patient. They encourage us to see each other beyond the surface and to recognize the needs in each other. We're less likely to criticize the mom with loud kids when we know what's going on in her home because we've heard the mom talk about it during group. We're less likely to be frustrated with the young woman who can't keep commitments when we find out she's been struggling with a job or school. We're more likely to offer support when we understand and care about what's going on with each other. That's a huge part of the atmosphere we create in the group.

Another important aspect of mentoring is that of equipping the younger women. As Missy said, within a Titus 2 group is an instant collection of shared knowledge and support. With such a rich variety of people and issues and life lessons going on, you're going to be able to store up knowledge and tools. You may not be dealing with every issue you hear about—you may not have kids or a husband or job troubles. But later, when something does come along in your life, you'll remember those conversations and realize you're not the only woman who's ever gone through it. You'll be better equipped than others who've never heard of or had an inkling they might experience that issue one day. And who knows, you may one day be able to offer your own suggestions and insights based on a particular season in your life.

I sometimes tell a story that had a great impact on me and my approach to Titus 2–based mentoring ministries. I used to be a guidance counselor and through that would attend a workshop every year. There was another woman who did the same, and as time went by we became close friends and chose to room together each year. We were good long-distance pals, but although we talked several times a year by phone or e-mail, we looked forward to that week when we could catch up with each other in person. Just like girls, we'd sit and talk for hours and share about our lives, filling each other in on the big events of the past year as well as the day-to-day moments.

I remember like it was yesterday when I told her about our Titus 2 groups and all the friends I have now because of them—women across generations. I shared about the Bible studies and life lessons and how wonderful the fellowship was. I talked about how rewarding it was to see the impact these relationships had on all the women. And I talked about how I now had a dozen close friends I could call anytime to pray over the phone with whenever I needed their support.

To be honest, I talked as though everybody has what I had.

My friend looked at me in silence for a moment. Then she asked, "Are you serious? You have friends who would do that?" She shook her head and sadly admitted, "I don't have a single friend like that."

For a moment I didn't know what to say. To me that was inconceivable. But I rallied myself. "Well then, you go back home and work on finding friends who will partner with you and pray with you! It's not hard. You know you have some close friends. You just need to work at taking it to the next step. You'll be so blessed."

"But how do I do that?" she asked.

Again I was shocked. I couldn't understand how someone my age, as intelligent as she was, as involved in her church family as she was, did not know how to find and foster the sorts of relationships we talk about in this book. She was a professional who worked with and even mentored others for a living. How was it possible?

Thankfully, I was able to talk more with her and give her some insights into how to make it happen. And I trust she went home and set about doing that. If she did, I'm certain she began something transformational in her life and hopefully in her church community.

Dear reader, I say the same thing to you that I did to her: make it happen. It isn't that hard. You know you have women around you who would join you. You know you have the resources. There may already be a similar ministry or program set up where you live. However the path to it, a Titus 2 ministry will give you more support and love and interaction than you ever dreamed of. My prayer is that you will find such an outlet to bless you richly. As Missy and the others sharing their stories have said, it is a must for a healthy and fulfilled life.

Heart Check

> And let us consider how we may spur one
> another on toward love and good deeds, not giv-
> ing up meeting together, as some are in the habit
> of doing, but encouraging one another—and all
> the more as you see the Day approaching.
>
> —Hebrews 10:24-25

Have you ever really considered what you'd get out of a mentoring relationship? What did you envision?

_____

_____

_____

_____

What is something that happened in your life that you wished you'd had a group of peers and mentors to help you with? How might the situation have turned out differently?

_____

_____

_____

_____

What do you feel you could offer other women in the way of support? Explain.

_____

_____

_____

_____

Father, I know Your goal for us is to have not only instruction from women but support and love and guidance. I crave that in my life. Help me as I seek out like-minded women so that we can be richly blessed together.

It is amazing what a small group of women can accomplish when they work together. Through our Titus 2 ministry I have seen many women using their talents and doing things to help further the kingdom. One of the reasons, I think, is that there's an understanding of how important it is for women to be close. Our women know each other intimately through the meetings and what they share, and that feeling of togetherness spills out into other avenues of our lives. You won't get that kind of connection with people you don't share with—and you won't share with people you don't know.

Have you ever gone up to a perfect stranger to confide in her about something that is very personal to you? I doubt it. Why? Because it's important to know that the person you confide in will honor your privacy and keep what you tell her in confidence. The women in our small groups know that whatever is said in our discussions is confidential and will not be repeated. Trust is very important in our society today. There are so many things that can happen in our lives, and sometimes we just need a caring and listening ear. But we've got to feel like what we say stays in the room. Our women have that trust.

And it shows in the energy among the ladies—in the excitement and the way they go out into the church community still holding on to their trust and each other. I have seen nothing but positive results with our small groups. During the meeting season the ladies talk and laugh together often as they build up their relationships. The young ones can't wait to share with other women not in their group all that they have learned or done that month. The older ones are always chatting and planning the next meeting. Different age groups talk together more often, fellowship together, go out together, and help out with kids or other needs. It brings such energy to the church.

I'm ashamed to say I hardly knew some of the younger ladies in our church when we started, other than to speak to them here and there, usually a hello before or after service. Now, after having several different young ladies in my group, I know them so much better. They're no longer strangers but dear friends. You get to know all the women in the group on a personal level. You know about their families and what is important to them. You know their dreams and their ambitions. You know who needs encouragement and what gifts they have that they've never shared.

For all these reasons and more, this program is priceless, and I'm so thankful for the opportunity to see and be a part of it—God's vision for women. What a precious gift they are receiving—the gifts of mentoring and wisdom and compassion that the older women can give to younger women and the gifts of openness and drive to grow that the younger can give to the older. I have learned so much in my interactions with our young women, and I'm grateful to have found a way to know them better. We're all blessed by our Titus 2 relationships.

—JULIE, MENTOR

One of the best things about our small groups is the opportunity to be involved with women whom we never would have known otherwise. Especially those mature ladies who are mentoring us. I'll be honest: without the groups, I never would have gotten to know them. And to now be with these ladies and watch them step out because they were challenged to lead, to see them share from their lives, has been amazing. And it's made me realize that, regardless of how hard it may be for me to share, if they can do it, I know I can.

And I can see how other girls feel the same way. There have been many times when we have girls in our group nobody really knows much about at all. And then you get a conversation going and you start finding things out about them that you never would've known or expected. And suddenly you connect and you become friends.

Sometimes it takes awhile for this to happen. Part of it is being scared of what people are going to think of you and what you've done and been through. We all experience that. But we learn that we're covered by grace and we can give it to God and reveal it to each other. And then we tell each other, "It's okay. It's really okay." Within our groups we have the opportunity to receive or offer support and advice and love and prayer. It absolutely makes the pain or fear of sharing worth it!

But I've also learned something else: when not to share. I don't mean because I don't want to admit anything. I mean that as I've gotten older and hopefully wiser from the counsel of these amazing ladies, I've learned that my opinion isn't the most important one in the room. It's okay to be quiet and listen to what others say. If I just sit back, then somebody else can sit up and take that step in faith of revealing her heart. It gives others an opportunity to grow, and it gives me an opportunity to offer my support. Seeing that—watching other women grow in their relationships and faith, and being able to be on the giving end of encouragement—has been very cool to experience.

Perhaps the craziest thing I've seen is that because of my own experiences with life and with the groups, I've had some of the younger women looking to me to mentor them. They come to me because they know I've been through a lot. And that's true: I do have plenty of life experiences to share. But I never in a million years would have thought I'd be someone other girls would want advice from! That just goes to show how amazing a Titus 2 ministry can be—that I have learned enough to begin helping others. It's a great feeling.

—MINDY, MENTEE

CHAPTER THREE

OPEN DOORS

Hospitality Is As Hospitality Does

> Hospitality means we take people into
> the space that is our lives and our minds
> and our hearts and our work and our
> efforts. Hospitality is the way we come
> out of ourselves. It is the first step towards
> dismantling the barriers of the world.
> Hospitality is the way we turn a prejudiced
> world around, one heart at a time.
> —*Joan Chittister*

LAUREN AND BEVERLY'S STORY

LAUREN. Beverly and I came to a Titus 2 ministry about ten years ago when we were asked to be mentors. At the time, we both wondered how it would work out. (Let us reassure you: it worked out wonderfully!) And we were coming from different places in our lives. I craved something more to occupy me. I was an empty nester with kids grown and gone. But I felt like I had so much nurturing left inside me. I craved more interaction with the younger generation. And even though I wasn't quite sure how I'd do in a leadership position, I was certain this adventure would fill that void in me. So I was ready to go—full steam ahead. I was excited at the thought of working with young women. Truly excited.

BEVERLY. I, on the other hand, was struggling with some difficult issues at home. To be honest, at the time, I felt completely inadequate to fill the role of mentor. I was under pressure, I was failing as a mom (at least that's how I felt), so how could I be entrusted with the care of a whole group of young women? It couldn't possibly work out, could it?

Well, it was tough, and it took some prayer and serious decision-making, but in the end I accepted the challenge. It was scary. I just had to keep reminding myself that despite a season of heartache, I had something of value to offer. And I did. I'd made it through the raising of our kids—the good and the bad—and I had wisdom to share. Lessons of the heart such as staying faithful in the storms of life. That was something I had firsthand experience with. But also life lessons. As it turned out, Lauren and I both found a real need in these young ladies for practical life skills.

LAUREN. Yes! As we worked through the lessons at each meeting, we spent a lot of time talking about faith and how that related to our daily lives—how the living out of our faith looked in terms of our actions toward others. We focused on how to be the best wife, mom, and friend we could. We show those characteristics in many ways by how we cherish the loved ones in our lives—and for some that comes easily. But we discovered that, for many of the young women in our group, it did *not* come easily. Some of these women didn't know how to show love through the nurturing of others. They had no idea how to be thoughtful and consider others' needs in the little day-to-day moments we all encounter. For whatever reason, they'd never been taught some important practical lessons of the home. So we made it our mission to show them.

BEVERLY. One of the best ways to show others how to do something is to do it yourself through modeling. So that's what we did (and that's what we still do). Through our actions we demonstrated behaviors and skills by taking them into our homes and "loving on them," as the saying goes. We served them meals, cleaned up after them, doted on them. We gave them little gifts. We showed them with our words and deeds that they were special to us and worthy of attention. And it was a joy to see how our girls flourished under that.

Again, our purpose was to teach while we mothered. We weren't just serving dinner; we were showing them how to cook and set a table and host guests in the home. There were so many lessons to be learned!

For instance, one year I had a tea party for my girls. I sent out formal invitations by mail. Then I put together a delightful spread for them—nice table settings, great food, the works. I collected dresses and accessories for any girls who might come without them and had everything ready to go.

When the young women arrived, into the "dressing room" they went, choosing outfits, changing, rummaging through the makeup and supplies, curling or straightening their hair. They giggled and fixed themselves up and then emerged like butterflies to enjoy the meal. And they had an amazing time. They put on airs and really played it up and enjoyed the food and everything. One of them said, "I've never been to anything like a tea party before in my life!" And it meant the world to me that I was able to make that happen for her—something so simple but so meaningful.

The other side of that is I was also able to give them some valuable lessons. I talked to them about the logistics of how to set a table for guests. And I let them know that I didn't have enough dishes to complete my table settings for the party. Did that stop me from inviting folks over? No, I asked friends and neighbors to let me borrow what I needed. I explained to the group that hospitality means you never worry that you don't have enough or that it isn't good enough. Inviting others into your home is a gift to them—the gift of your attention, not your silverware.

We're always saying that you can serve hot dogs on paper plates just as easily as you can serve steak on china. In many aspects it's our way of teaching them that it's the care that matters, not the details. And the girls get it. Just like the night of the tea party, you can see them taking that lesson in and realizing they can throw their own parties.

LAUREN. Not only that, but we teach them all the other little pieces that go along with hospitality. Things like RSVP'ing for our Titus 2 meetings each month so that they'll learn and remember to RSVP for other social engagements. It's such a small thing, but an RSVP can make a huge difference to someone trying to plan a meal or event, so we want them to be mindful of that.

And things like party favors—special take-home gifts we provide. It's something that lets the young women know we planned ahead, thought about them, and are glad they've come to our homes. And it's something they can do for their own guests. Again, some of our girls have never been taught to think of those little things that express affection and appreciation. So we talk about being thoughtful about those who give of themselves and not taking this blessing for granted. Teaching kindness, consideration, and simple things like using manners is something we model, as well as talk about, in our groups. In a way, we're the mothers some of these girls have never had.

And it's working. The longer we've done this, and the longer the younger ladies have been exposed to the ministry of hospitality, the more it's becoming second nature for them to respond in kind—both on the giving and receiving ends. They're doing things they never have before. Things some of them never expected they could or would do. Many are beginning to open up their own homes to friends, hosting them without shame. Many are now leading "house churches." They're making crafts. They're cooking. They're signing up and taking meals to new moms when they get home from the hospital. They're feeling confident enough in their skills to start taking a role in serving others—they're welcoming it and becoming excited at the possibilities and opportunities. It's been amazing to see how we're changing the course of a generation who otherwise might not have learned hospitality. And it's rewarding to know they'll then pass these skills on to their children.

One of the strongest messages of our focus is that by thinking of others and fostering relationships, these ladies are building up a base of support for themselves. They are arming themselves with practical skills that help them be a support for their family and friends. We all need women we can call on when a need arises in our lives. We want someone who loves God and who will stand beside us. These women, through our Titus 2 mentoring, are building that network of caring support.

BEVERLY. Many younger women today are separated from meaningful connections with mentoring women— often their mothers. They're separated by location or broken homes or painful pasts. They're separated by the busyness of everyday life. These women need someone to help teach them not only how to live life God's way but how to live life successfully. But many do not have a godly person in their lives to remind them what Jesus wants for their future, much less how to live life with intention and with others in mind. Through our Titus 2 ministry we're giving them that model.

And we're creating bonds between women. Some of them—including me—might otherwise have never shared a meal with each other. (And I feed a bunch of folks at my table, so that's saying a lot.) We might never have become friends because of our different ages and stages of life and living in different social circles. Now we do know each other, and I mean really *know* each other. Through hospitality and through the life lessons and spiritual lessons we share, we're getting below surface conversations and interactions to the real us. As our relationships develop, we're learning we don't have to hide and cover our deepest needs. And that level of trust stays with us too. The relationships we make continue to bless us for years to come.

As humans, we're not designed to share with strangers. The bonds between the young and old, the scriptures explored, the discussions about life issues, the teaching moments—those things cannot occur via a casual "How are you?" in a church foyer, which is the only way many young women ever interact with the older generation in their churches. Only with time invested in each other do we reach a more intimate level.

LAUREN. And in the end, what we've done through our Titus 2 ministry has not only been great for the young ladies but equally wonderful for those of us who serve them. God instructed us to teach the young so that they can live faith-centered, meaningful lives. I think we've succeeded—but not just for the younger ones. We mentors also gain from the experience. We, too, enrich our lives. We don't look at it as something we have to do but something we love and look forward to. The way we see it, we're using the talents and gifts God gave us to teach our young women. They will one day be the older generation who will be instrumental in teaching and instructing the next generation. I am thankful I'm able to use the gift of hospitality that God blessed me with to help so many others on their life journeys.

What's been a true blessing to me is finding out these young women are so eager to be taught and trained. They're eager to learn life lessons and what God desires of them in their walk with Him. In our mentoring ministry, we come from very different backgrounds, social as well as economic. But we all gather with one thing passionately in common: our love of Jesus. I cannot adequately describe how rewarding that is for all of us in our Titus 2 program.

BEVERLY. And it's just plain fun! We enjoy thinking of ways we can give to our girls. One of our mentors makes recipe cards for the meals she cooks for each meeting. She gives them out to everyone each month, so that by the end of the year each young woman has a recipe file ready for company. Another mentor spends hours combing stores for perfect little gifts. She buys them in bulk and keeps them in a closet ready to go. According to whatever lesson has been taught at that month's meeting, she'll pull out a set and gift each of her mentees with one, so that the last thing those young women have as they walk out the door is a representation of their mentor's care and attention.

These lessons are important not just for them but for us older women as well. Yes, they're practical, but they also represent how precious we feel our group of ladies is. And how valued each one of them is to us individually. God holds them in high regard, and so do we. What we strive to do is represent His love to them.

Sometimes I look back at how unsure I felt when I first began my mentoring journey, and I have to laugh because I never should have doubted the impact God could have through me. It's a lesson I hope all my girls learn—that no matter how low their self-esteem or how little they think they may know, they can make an impact on another's life, simply by opening up and trusting that God will make use of her. What a gift that is.

Hospitality. It's a word that conveys many things. For one, a graciousness and a conscious awareness of others. For another, the giving of yourself through your deeds. In yet another way, the idea that you're putting someone's needs ahead of your own, even if just for a few hours. *Merriam-Webster's Dictionary* defines it as the "generous and friendly treatment of visitors and guests." That sounds pleasant, doesn't it?

Unfortunately, many of us have not yet had the opportunity to experience hospitality, either through giving or receiving. We don't know what it's like to be the focus of someone's attention. Or how it feels to make someone else the center for a while. In doing so, we've missed out on a crucial element of what should define us as women and Christians. That's a very sad state of affairs.

You may wonder why we put such an emphasis on hospitality. Consider this: In chapter 1, we talked about opening up and being vulnerable to a group of women. In chapter 2, we saw that doing so allows us to embrace the support and encouragement of our fellow group members—and offer our support in turn. Hospitality is a natural progression of this lesson. It is the physical representation of emotional support. It's not a chore, as Martha felt—the taking care of logistics. On the contrary, Jesus warned Martha, and us, that hospitality is a matter of the heart and not just appearances and actions. "Martha, . . . you are worried and upset about many things, but few things are needed—or indeed only one. Mary has chosen what is better, and it will not be taken away from her" (Luke 10:41–42).

Jesus taught that we are to care for one another. And He didn't mean only emotionally. "Love must be sincere," said Paul. "Share with the Lord's people who are in need. Practice hospitality" (Romans 12:9, 13). See that? Showing hospitality is *sharing* in another's life. That means contributing, making a significant difference in someone's life, doing something that sticks beyond a momentary action. True hospitality as Jesus taught extends into someone's life beyond the home's walls.

So, as a ministry that seeks to train young women in all aspects of the Christian life, it stands to reason a Titus 2 women's mentoring group would focus on serving others. We consider it vital—a mentoring ministry must include the caring, nurturing behavior and attitude of giving to one another through hospitality. In fact, I believe the heart of church growth is hospitality. The book of Acts tells us that in the early days of the church everybody met together in their homes and shared everything they had on a daily basis. And every day more and more people came to fellowship and share with each other.

Acts 2:47 says, "And the Lord added to their number daily." The writer intentionally added that the people met in their homes (v. 46). God wanted us to know that they met in the place most personal to these people. The way I envision it, outsiders were drawn to Christ and the church because of the hospitality and caring they saw in those early members of the faith. Those people had knowledge to impart to new believers, and they wanted to make sure they presented a welcoming home in which to do it. They were likely eager to do so.

Think about your own life. Many of you know about hospitality and have hopefully practiced it to some degree—or experienced others' hospitality toward you. But consider what it might be like to have access to a group of mature, experienced women with a lifetime of knowledge on the subject you could learn from. What if their goal, alongside mentoring you spiritually, was to give you access to that knowledge, intentionally sharing important information and personal insights? Recipes. Housekeeping tricks and organizational strategies. Sewing tips. How to host a baby shower. And be honest: wouldn't you love to learn how to neatly fold those annoying fitted sheets that always seem to get balled up in the corner of your linen closet?

What a harvest of information on living better!

Some of you may be thinking, *Hospitality just isn't my thing. I have other gifts, other ways to serve God. I'll leave the social aspects to someone else.* I ask you to reconsider. What may seem unnatural—or nerve-racking or even annoying—to you at first can quickly become a blessing as you learn what it feels like to sincerely minister to others.

Others of you may think, *I really don't have need of those skills right now. I'm not a wife. I'm not a mom. And I definitely don't need to know how to sew.* But someday you might. You never know what circumstances will come up in your future. Wouldn't it be great to have a head start on what you'll need? Trust me—the day your in-laws show up for Easter lunch is not the time to be experimenting on how to cook a nice meal. It is much nicer to be prepared.

All this is to say a Titus 2 mentoring group is so much more than a Bible study. Yes, feeding the spiritual side is important, as is feeding the relational component. But what rounds out a person is educating yourself in all facets of life. God wants each of us to be a complete woman. The whole package. And that's the point of mentoring: to impart wisdom in all aspects of your life, including practical and social skills. With a mentoring relationship, you have an inside track to a full library of knowledge.

And not just from the older women. The younger women can share insights as well. Each person has something she can contribute to the knowledge pool—perhaps something she learned from her mother or grandmother, perhaps something she never knew would be useful to others. Whatever the case, everyone's just a phone call or text away to answer your "hospitality emergency" questions. Who knows—at some point maybe you'll end up being the one with the quick answer or the "I've got you covered" reassurance. I promise you: that moment will be a fulfilling one for you!

My hope for you is that, as you explore a Titus 2 ministry, you will be richly blessed in many ways: spiritually, emotionally, relationally. And in ways that enhance your understanding of hospitality and the practical skills of life that allow you to minister to others in your own special ways. You won't be disappointed. In fact, your heart will be full.

Heart Check

Above all, love each other deeply, because love
covers over a multitude of sins. Offer hospitality to one another without grumbling. Each of
you should use whatever gift you have received
to serve others, as faithful stewards of God's
grace in its various forms.

—1 Peter 4:8–10

Have you ever considered the idea that mentoring relationships can go beyond the spiritual and emotional?
How does it make you feel to know you could have access
to practical insights as well?

_____

_____

_____

_____

What's a practical hospitality lesson you'd love to learn?
From your connections, whom do you picture teaching
you that skill?

_____

_____

_____

_____

Now that you think about it, do you have a life skill you could offer to someone else? Explain. From whom did you learn it?

_____

_____

_____

_____

God, You want me to be a whole woman, skilled in every aspect of my life so I can minister to others on many levels. Let me be an example of hospitality. Help me learn not just the spiritual but the practical lessons I need. Guide me to the women who are waiting to teach them to me.

Women throughout the ages have always had a need for relationships that offer strong, spiritual friendships and mentoring. Not only that, but there has always been a need for relationships that provide a template for life skills. Long ago, families shared homes and young women learned by example—either from their own families or the families they married into—how to be a wife, a mother, a caretaker for their family. They learned how to run a home. It was easy to do since they were surrounded by many multigenerational female members of that family and saw on a daily basis what was needed.

Today each family has their own home. The younger women are often busy with school or work or social activities and do not have time to learn the skills they will one day need. And once married, they often move away from the very ones who could help them develop these skills. Consequently, many of the younger generation do not really know how to cook, clean, manage their home, or raise a family. This often creates a crisis in the home as they struggle to provide what's necessary for a healthy marriage and sound child-rearing.

Thankfully, Titus 2 mentoring offers an opportunity for the same type of training many young women missed out on at home. It is a second chance to learn essential life skills from the older generation. Some of the mentoring women are their mothers' ages, while others are the age (or close to it) of their grandmothers. All of them have a wealth of information to share—things that may have been passed down for generations. So through their groups, the younger ones can learn valuable lessons from many different women with different backgrounds and different life experiences. They learn practical skills—all the ins and outs of running a home and family. But they learn other things as well. The most important of these is how to be a godly wife and mother.

Whatever the lesson, because of their small group, these young ladies now have someone to call when they need advice, counsel, or just a listening ear. And they develop friendships with women of all ages, not only their own. That's extremely important.

The best thing about Titus 2 mentoring is that it is for everyone. Nothing stands in the way. All women are welcome, young or old. No religious boundaries, no race boundaries, no socioeconomic boundaries. Simply support, love, and guidance for anyone who walks through the door. That's true hospitality.

—LISA, MENTOR

Real authenticity starts in our home. It doesn't start in the church; it starts where we live. We've got to let our barriers down and get out of our comfort zones, and we've got to be willing to have others come to our homes. We need to be uncomfortable, because it takes courage to be a person of God.

I remember when Jase and I were first married I had to make a big adjustment, something that was definitely outside my comfort zone. When I was growing up we didn't have people in our home. My dad's attitude was, "My home is my sanctuary, where I come back from work and rest." So that was the atmosphere that was fostered. We didn't have a lot of people over. It's not that we were unwelcoming. It's just that we didn't go out of our way to invite others. So when we had guests in our home, it was awkward. Very awkward. I grew up feeling that way.

And so when I got married and left to make my own home, I didn't know how to have others be a part of it. And of course I had to go and marry somebody completely the opposite from me. Jase's family's house is open to anybody, any time of the day or night. You don't knock; you just walk in and grab a plate. It was completely foreign to what I'd grown up with, so I had to watch and learn that attitude.

It wasn't easy. When I invited people to our house, or when we were hosting a small group, I would try to have everything perfect. And Jase would say, "What are you doing? You've got to make things comfortable. You can't have everything in its place. Some of these people are coming from nothing. You've got to meet them where they are."

He was right, of course. And so I had to quit. It took awhile, but I've come a long way since then.

All this is to say, hospitality doesn't come naturally to many. So it was a lifesaver to me that it was such a focus in our small group. Our mentors went out of their way to pamper us and teach us. They had a fun side to things too. For example, they always sent us home with something. With one of the groups, we would leave every time with recipe cards they had typed out for each of us. The card included everything they'd cooked that night. I still have my little box of cards, and I still fix "Aunt Carol's Crunch Salad."

Another mentor would give out a door prize, just a little something special. Another had a closet no one else was allowed to touch. She filled it with everything. I mean everything—twelve of everything. It was like a treasure chest. And when the night was over she'd pull something out of there and we'd all be like, "Oooh, what are we going to get?"

Because of the care these women gave us—not just the hospitality and practical lessons but the extra attention—all of us younger ladies couldn't wait to show up. That's something a lot of us said. We loved getting off work and getting a babysitter and running from soccer practice in whatever we had on, just to make it to group. We didn't even have to think about what to bring—no potluck or dessert. The whole atmosphere the mentors worked to create was one in which it was all about caring and nurturing and supporting their girls. And it was a real treat.

—MISSY, MENTEE

CHAPTER FOUR

OPEN HANDS

Compassion in a Me-Centered World

> If we are to love our neighbors, before doing anything else we must see our neighbors. With our imagination as well as our eyes, that is to say like artists, we must see not just their faces but the life behind and within their faces. Here it is love that is the frame we see them in.
>
> —*Frederick Buechner*

JAMIE'S STORY

Our Titus 2 ministry started at my church at the perfect time for me in my faith journey. My husband of six years and I had just had our first baby, a precious little boy. As you can imagine, it was a whirlwind time of learning how to be parents, sleepless nights and busy days, and coping with the many changes that come to a marriage when a tiny new person is introduced to the household. It was one of the most tiring times of my life and of course one of the most rewarding, as I learned what it meant to be a mother.

What should have been a completely joyous season, however, was marred by something completely unexpected and unwelcome: my dad made the choice to leave our family and my mom after thirty-nine years. He had found someone else he loved, he said, and he was going to make a life with her. So he packed his things and left.

I can't describe to you how shocked and hurt we all were. My mom, of course, was hit the hardest. After discussing the options, my husband and I decided to offer our own home as a refuge for her. This wasn't a light decision, and it wasn't easy to make happen either. We had a small house and a newborn. My mom had to sleep on the couch, and we all had to make adjustments in our usual living patterns. For me, who was already juggling the whole new-mommy thing, it was stressful. Especially when having my mom so physically close opened me up to her emotions on a very personal level. I couldn't do any less. I loved her and wanted to support her. But it was hard.

So that was the scenario into which Titus 2 arrived in my life. I was eager to start attending the group meetings, but I was also a bit apprehensive about how I'd handle things. I won't lie—it was an emotional time in my life.

I never should have worried.

I remember clearly the first meeting we all had together. We made our introductions, going around the table. At first it was the usual short-and-sweet bios—spouses, kids, jobs, etc. We were all a bit unsure of each other and just how much to expose. But gradually, as each woman shared and the others gave their input and made comparisons, more details began to come out. And somehow, in the course of that, the topic got onto memories of our fathers.

Oh my goodness. What were the odds of that? Before I knew it, I was overcome with emotion. I couldn't hold back the tears as I shared with my new group what I was going through. I'm sure it was not a pretty sight. And it could have been a very awkward moment—not only for me but for those women around me who were more or less seeing me break down in front of them. Some of these women were complete strangers to me.

But that wasn't the case. In a flash, I was immediately surrounded by the group. As I shared, they gathered around me and loved on me, rubbed my shoulder, hugged me, let me know they were there for me. They gave me their full attention—a gift in itself in a world where it's hard to focus on others for more than a second. They waited patiently as I dragged out all the hurtful details I'd been trying to keep hidden away. Then they comforted me and told me it was okay. They pushed aside the shame I felt at what my dad had done. They pushed aside the shame at how angry and hurt I was (because aren't we supposed to be forgiving and not harbor resentment?). The shame at how weary I was trying to help my mom. They validated all my feelings and accepted me where I was. They told me they'd help me through it.

I can't explain how freeing that was. Truly, wonderfully freeing. And I could see how others were affected by that unconditional acceptance. Tears were shed by everyone together. And as the ice was broken, other ladies shared stories of their own struggles and received the benefit of our group's encouragement and love. Our mentors facilitated it beautifully. It was an exhausting but incredible experience as we ran the gamut of emotions.

But what a blessing! Because we experienced this together—and especially because this time of sharing happened at the very first meeting—we instantly became a close-knit group. There were no walls—they'd been toppled right from the get-go. We might not have shared every single thing about ourselves, but we knew that if we could expose the things we did, expose the heartaches and pains, to relative strangers at the first meeting, without any fear of rejection or repercussion, then we for sure had a safe place in which to share things down the road. Anything at all. Unconditionally.

And so, in spite of what was one of the most heart-breaking times of my life, that year became one of my most precious. Not only in terms of all I experienced as a new mom, but because of my Titus 2 ladies. With them, I was uplifted time and time again, each month we met. And as my mother dealt with difficult issues of her own, and rightfully focused on her needs and building a new life for herself physically and emotionally, my mentors (and peers too) became my surrogate moms. They were there to encourage me, guide me, teach me, and pray for me. I would come home rejuvenated by my group and knowing that I was going to make it through, which helped me better help my mother and be the wife and mother my husband and son needed. It helped me forgive my dad and forgive myself for the resentment I'd harbored and allowed to depress me—even when I didn't show it to others.

Our Titus 2 small group was so much more than what I'd expected. I thought we'd get together each month and share a meal and a laugh, have a bit of Bible study. And all of those things are important. But those sweet women also provided godly models during a time when I was not able to lean on my own mother. I cherish those relation-ships and still keep in touch with mentors and friends from that group, even as I've moved on to new ones.

I think my favorite meetings were the ones held in one particular mentor's home. She owned a tiny townhome with a kitchen table for four. So four of us gals would cram around the table and the rest would gather on sev-eral bar stools and the nearby couch. And in spite of the close quarters, we would have the best time together. It didn't matter to our mentor, nor to us, that she didn't have a big home and lots of comfy couches or fancy furnish-ings. It wasn't necessary. That gracious woman showed us hospitality in her casual, cozy home, and we were all blessed by her.

Not only that, she taught us about emotional hospitality by being honest with us regarding her life and circumstances and allowing us to do the same with her and each other. She had been married four times, and she revealed many hurts to us. But she always made clear she was earnestly seeking God in the midst of it all. And her openness in our group created an inviting, unintimidating environment in which to share anything we ourselves might be struggling with and receive the blessing of encouragement from women who had "been there." She was an inspiring model of what it meant to foster an outward view rather than a self-centered one.

Compassion was a huge part of our small groups. That's important, because compassion is what deepens our friendships. And it is so important for women in the church to be friends. As companions within the body of Christ, we are connected in ways that others aren't. "Therefore, as we have opportunity, let us do good to all people, especially to those who belong to the family of believers," says Galatians 6:10. God calls us to "do good," to take care of each other as the family of believers and to minister to each other's needs. As we share our lives, we open the doors to our vulnerable selves, the part that needs Him most. And when we can talk about what He's doing in our lives, when we realize and are open about our weaknesses with each other, that's when the most powerful lessons are learned and the most strength taken from each other.

I especially love that our Titus 2 groups allow us to experience compassion and emotional vulnerability with women we might never have connected with otherwise. That's one of the benefits of our small groups—we are forced to meet new women outside our usual circles, encouraged to bond with those not of our age group or social setting or work environment. By doing so, we're given a whole new level of support. What I mean is that we tend to spend our time with like-minded people, those who share the same likes and dislikes, the same passions and interests. Those are our friends, and we're generally good about meeting together and spending time with each other. We naturally seek each other out.

This happens far less frequently with those with whom we don't share an apparent connection. If we're honest, we'll admit we certainly don't make it a priority to spend time with those who aren't our close friends, with those who don't run in our circles, with those who are Sunday-morning acquaintances.

Without organized small groups, therefore, we wouldn't have the chance to befriend and trust women we might otherwise have never met. And we'd miss out on a whole new perspective. Many perspectives! Having the opportunity to put something out there and have it examined by such a wide variety of ladies opens you up to a lot of different viewpoints and suggestions. You have to get used to making yourself vulnerable to them. But the rewards are worth it.

And really, although we might at first assume we have nothing in common—different ages, different places in life, marriage, family—what we too often forget is that we have the most important connection of all to each other: our faith. All the rest is secondary to this sister-making fact. Small groups bring us together, united by our faith in God and the love of Jesus. Small groups turn the most unlikely matchups into dear friends. And they allow us the gift of entering into each other's lives and making a difference.

I love Jamie's story because it gets to the heart of what so many of us crave. We need emotional connections, especially as women. While we can and hopefully do find those connections fairly easily within our families and our close friends, it's not as simple in the general church congregation. As we've seen time and time again, we tend to gravitate toward those who are most like us— the same ages, the same family or marriage circumstances, the same jobs and interests. And there's nothing wrong with that. We gain a lot from those relationships.

But we need to understand and actively work at making those connections *outside* our inner circles. That's not as easy as it would seem.

Churches do work at this to some degree. They seek to provide connectedness through a variety of methods that build relationships between members. As we've seen, the most successful method involves small groups that meet regularly. Small groups provide a more efficient and friendlier way of getting to know others in a large congregation—and even in smaller ones.

But think about it: most groups in churches focus on a specific need or issue or demographic—everything from Bible study to service projects. I've belonged to churches where members get together to care for the sick or aging, provide food or therapy services for individuals and couples, and set up activities for children and teens. I've been a part of churches that have divorce and grief recovery programs, alcohol and drug addictions recovery groups, singles groups, and special groups for those with sexual addictions and eating disorders. And just about every possibility of people-caring group you can imagine.

Most of them, however, cater to a specific group of people who tend to be like-minded or who are facing the same situations. And sometimes their focus is outward rather than inward. So while they're well intentioned and God ordained and absolutely have purpose and meaning to the participants, they're still dividing people by interests or needs.

So we need to dig deeper, don't we? How do we begin to encourage small group membership across a more diverse spectrum of our churches? And more to the point, how do we specifically meet the needs of *women* across generations, across social, economic, marital, and any other boundaries? Pretty intentionally, actually. You'd have to, to bring together such a diverse group.

As you've seen, that's exactly what a Titus 2 women's mentoring ministry does. Not only that, but it specifically chooses to take the group out of the church and place it into homes. Home groups are by far the most successful type of small group. It is in a home that believers can welcome others with the blessing of Christian hospitality. And hospitality, as we have seen, extends our embrace of others personally and intimately by opening up our private physical spaces—the places where we live, eat, dress, and sleep. Inviting friends to participate in our lives, in our houses, is an instant way of relating.

Let's dig further, shall we? An even deeper, richer approach to hospitality is when we open our *hearts* to each other. We take the physical welcome we just talked about and we make it more—an emotional kindness and generous warmth that we extend to our friends.

I would like for you to consider the idea that small group hospitality goes beyond the physical to the emotional. You must know that to do this there are heart costs involved. Challenges. When we share our lives with each other, we give of our time. Our energy. And it requires relational risks. We give parts of ourselves away. But this is what we must do as Christians: love each other in radical ways, go above and beyond, stretch our boundaries and move outside our defined boxes. No, it's not always easy to do so. Or comfortable. But we are called as women to be in a relationship of influence with one another, and that can only happen when we're open to each other.

A Titus 2 small group offers a space for you to pour out your hurts, the pain of your abuse or addiction or abandonment, the fears of marriage and parenting. And a space to know it is a burden now shared. I use that phrase intentionally. When we share ourselves with each other, we are shouldering part of each other's burdens. Picture it literally if you like—imagine your pain as a big block. When you expose your true self to the women in your group, you're offering that block to them. They pass it around, one to another, and they each tear off a piece of it, until your block returns to you significantly lighter and smaller than before.

I give you this analogy not to trivialize anyone's hurts but to offer a visual of what emotional hospitality entails. It is a powerful tool. Through sharing, we break another's pain into pieces. Again and again, woman by woman, we accept and reduce the burden to a fraction of the original. No, it doesn't make the pain magically disappear. But hopefully the weight of it on your soul is lessened by knowing you are surrounded by those who are there to help you. That's the miracle of compassion, the miracle of empathy. We simply need to condition ourselves to embrace those opportunities to draw closer to God and to one another.

Jamie agrees. "I don't consider myself a weak person. I am strong in my faith. And so even during the hardest days after my dad left and my mom came to stay with us, I could have made it. I would have prayed for the strength to make it day by day, and I know eventually God would have made sure I got there. But it was so much easier to simply take my pain and share it with my group, knowing they were there with me. I received so much strength from them—more than I ever would have had on my own! And in return I was able to stand shoulder to shoulder in support of other women in the group. We all shared each other's burdens."

Jamie makes a great point. There's the receiving side of emotional hospitality that she initially experienced. There's also the giving side that she was later able to experience. A Titus 2 ministry teaches us how to become aware of others and to meet their needs. Consider this: as hard as it may be for you to open up, it's equally as hard for the others in your group. If you take the time to consider it, you probably know exactly what they're thinking:

- *I hate seeming weak. I don't want others to criticize me or to pity me.*
- *If I were to talk about personal things, I'm afraid it would turn into the newest gossip.*
- *I hate giving others an opening to say something that trivializes the pain of what I'm going through.*

- *I know people would never look at and feel about me the same if they knew this about me.*
- *It hurts too much to talk about it.*

These are the things many of us tell ourselves in an effort to hide, when we seek to keep from truly exposing our hurts to the light. They are not just excuses. They are legitimate reasons why we are hesitant to talk about, or refuse to talk about, our deepest losses, pains, burdens, and fears. But through our small groups, we have the opportunity to push ourselves. And the opportunity to foster vulnerability in others. It's a sweet moment for a woman to feel she is the singular focus of a whole group's undivided attention. It honors her commitment to be open. And it shows her that no matter what, others stand with her.

My friend, we *must* work to overcome those fears that emotionally separate us from each other. We *must* find that place where we are comfortable sharing, where the overwhelming compassion from those around us melts away the walls. Small groups provide that safe haven. Here are several reasons:

- Small groups allow women to unconditionally support you in a way that demonstrates, "I won't walk away when your burden troubles me. I'll seek God's help, for both of us. I will walk this tough road with you."
- Small groups provide a space of confidentiality where discretion is honored. You can count on them to keep silent about things shared privately.
- Small groups provide counsel and guidance among friends of all ages and backgrounds. As a collective

experience, they have seen it all. So they don't give up when you're having a rough time.

- Small group members stand in the gap and give you courage to be strong. They hold up your arms when you cannot be brave yourself. They rally around you and provide the support and love you and your family need during tough times.

- Small group members are the prayer partners who will take you to the Lord immediately and often.

Walking through trials with Christian sisters, if they are true friends in the faith, strengthens the bond of our relationships like no other experience. Ecclesiastes 4:12 says, "Though one may be overpowered, two can defend themselves. A cord of three strands is not quickly broken." There is nothing equal to the shared understanding of tightrope-walking a crisis that will reinforce our commitment to one another.

And troubles and trials will happen to all of us; there's no getting around that. What we go through to mature in Christ is a testing. Sometimes it's our daily troubles, such as parenting demands or tough days on the job. Sometimes it's a terrible thing such as divorce or job loss. A heartache, a death, an illness, an unexpected setback—we know these equalizers of life are inevitable. Dealing with those hardships alone, however, does not have to be. And for us as God's women, it should not be. We can wallow in our pain and self-pity or we can be there for one another. We can protect ourselves or we can risk whatever it takes and reach out to each other. We can be emotionally closed off or emotionally compassionate to our sisters in Christ.

My prayer is that you will not often need to avail yourselves of another's compassionate response to pain. But if and when that time arrives, I pray you will have the support of a Titus 2 mentoring group. If so, I know you will emerge stronger and wiser and better able to return the favor.

Heart Check

Carry each other's burdens, and in this way
you will fulfill the law of Christ. . . . The one who
receives instruction in the word should share all
good things with their instructor.

—Galatians 6:2, 6

Have you ever considered the idea of emotional hospitality?
What do you think of the concept?

_____

_____

_____

_____

Has there been a time in your life when you needed to
unburden yourself but didn't? How did that make you
feel? Explain.

_____

_____

_____

_____

If you had an opportunity to show emotional hospitality to someone you know has a need, who would that be? What would you do or say to encourage her?

_____

_____

_____

_____

God, one of the hardest things for us as women is to share from the hidden places of our hearts. Help me be open to doing so and receiving the gift of another's compassion. Help me do the same, knowing it is a representation of Your love for her.

I didn't have a lot of friends while I was growing up. I always felt different around the other children in school. I was definitely a bit of a loner.

That began to change when I went to college. Through a family connection, I started to go to a campus ministry center. And it was there that I began to really understand the Bible. I eventually gave my life to Christ. And I met people who were genuinely nice and kind.

Then I met a great guy through the center, whom I ended up marrying soon after graduating college. When we started going to a new church, I leaped at the chance to join a women's group I had heard about. I didn't really understand it was a mentoring group; I thought it was just for women to get to know each other. But I was so hungry for friends that it didn't matter to me.

I met several younger women like me at our first meeting and even some a little older. When a woman who was close to my age introduced herself, it just felt like we were going to be friends. That was one need I had that our Titus 2 program filled.

But then something else happened that night. I had another need I didn't even realize. We were sitting around the table for our meal, answering questions in a "get to know you" exercise. The questions were fairly simple to respond to. At least they seemed to be. This was mine: "Do you have a favorite summer family vacation memory from when you were younger than ten?" Pretty painless question.

Well, I don't know what came over me. It might have been a kindness I'd sensed among the women there. Or maybe it was something someone else had shared. But I just teared up because the memories that simple question brought up were painful.

My parents split up when I was very young, and I never had a relationship with my dad. I never had any family vacations. And it was painful to remember that.

That night, as the memories overwhelmed me, I opened up and shared with the group. They began to encourage me. One of my mentors hugged me and said a prayer for me. And the prospective friend I had met earlier came over and sat by me. Then she took my hand and held it the rest of the time we sat at the table.

They were wonderful to me. I was a bit embarrassed, but I felt so accepted that feeling soon went away. Then I begin to sense the pain lifting. And, for the first time, I began to see what true Christian friendship looked like.

I am so grateful for my mentors for opening up their homes to me and to many like me. Without their care for me—who didn't really trust anyone very much—I would be stuck. I'm certain of that. Stuck in church. Trying to do the right thing, but without understanding God's love, mercy, and grace. That is what those women, my friends (yes, I have quite a few now, including the dear one who held my hand that night), have shown me. Although my family was broken, I have a forever family now that has helped me heal. They love me and care for me.

I am glad I have the chance to say how blessed I am that God gave me my Titus 2 group.

—LAURIE*

*Name changed by request.

I love what our Titus 2 ministry provides for our women! Those who participated in my small group this past year, and every year, seem to be more aware of each other. We are a big church, and gathering in smaller group settings helps us reduce the sense of being overwhelmed by numbers. We can be more intimate in our small groups, so we feel more comfortable sharing about our concerns or victories. Women who did not know each other well or at all before are now greeting one another and talking more. We all feel more connected.

I definitely see differences in how younger women in my group have interacted with the older women. Our group has ministered to single, professional ladies from college age to early thirties for the past three years. One young lady in particular comes to mind. Her mother doesn't live close by, so this young lady seemed to be dejected when our meetings finished for that particular year. She had friends but is a very quiet woman, so I wasn't sure she'd reach out to them. I felt I needed to form a closer relationship with her, so I reached out to her.

We have carried on that friendship to this day. We meet every couple of weeks or once a month for lunch. We remember each other's birthdays. We check up on each other. The friendship has been a blessing to both of us. She now interacts with all the mentors in our group and even approaches others to sit with during Bible classes. She is more interested in and outgoing with the older women. I think this is something that probably occurs in all the small groups. Bonds are made that are very special.

Women who are in small groups in churches are powerhouses of ministry. The women who know each other in these groups are constantly calling on each other to help with different needs for members of our church as well as for each other. We all have times of joy and times of trial. We uphold one another in prayer to the Lord.

For me personally, to know there are ladies close to me who pray with me and for my family and me when those times come is such a comfort. I appreciate having a group of women I know well enough that I can call on them when it is time to celebrate—and even more important, when there is a time of pain and difficulty. I believe God wants these relationships to show us His love and concern for us. We are His love shown to others.

My Titus 2 ministry has helped me grow in so many ways. I've become more outgoing. More aware of other women around me and their needs. I've made many friends and hope to make many more. I'm working on trying to be the woman God wants me to be. I needed to stretch and grow, and our small groups have been my catalyst. I'm so thankful I've had this opportunity.

I am most thankful, though, to have had the opportunity to foster these same lessons, these same joys, in the young women I host in my home. To know they are learning important lessons about life and faith—ones that will serve them well for many years to come—has made it all worthwhile. I cherish my time with these precious ladies.

—JUDY, MENTOR

CHAPTER FIVE

OPEN MINDS

Study, Study, Study the Word of God

I want to know one thing, the way to heaven: how to land safe on that happy shore. God himself has condescended to teach the way; for this very end he came from heaven. He hath written it down in a book. O give me that book! At any price give me the Book of God! I have it: here is knowledge enough for me. . . . In his presence I open, I read his book; for this end, to find the way to heaven.

—*John Wesley*

CONNIE'S STORY

I came from a family that attended church during my younger years but in no way brought church home with us. My parents felt it was up to the church and not them to provide my spiritual education—but since it wasn't reflected at home, there was pretty much no way to grow spiritually. By age fifteen we were attending church less and less and soon not at all. So I went on my merry way without God in the picture. And that's how I spent my life all the way through school and marriage. It wasn't until I was older and a wife with children that God finally called me to Him.

When my husband and I became Christians, we joined a church and regularly attended services, drinking in the lessons learned there. We were fellowshipping with others, learning a lot. But still, for me, something was missing. I very much enjoyed the worship services, the music, and learning from the sermons. I enjoyed the people. But I wasn't really getting fed the way I knew I wanted to be. I'm one of those insatiable learner types and I craved more. I just wasn't sure how to get that "more."

So I tried reading my new Bible. You can imagine how that went. I had no frame of reference and no background knowledge of the stories and lessons contained in it, no real concept other than that the first part was the *really* old stuff and the second part was where the red Jesus words showed up. I'd thumb through those thin, crackly pages, desperately trying to gather something from them. But it was like reading a different language, a mysterious book that I could page through and understand a word of here and there, but not really comprehend as a whole. And I very much wanted to.

I even tried taking my Bible to church so that I could follow along when our pastor read the scriptures before and during his sermon. But as you might guess, by the time I found where he was reading from (that desperate rifling of pages: *Does John come before or after James? Oh, wait—there are three, no, four Johns! Which one? Shoot, now he's reading from Paul. I don't see the book of Paul anywhere . . .*), he was long gone to the next thing.

So for a time I gave up on my dream of in-depth Bible study and focused on other things. I was still growing in my faith, of course. Still joyful at what I'd found in Christ after all these years. Still thankful that my husband was on this journey with me. And I was reading books on spiritual growth and Christian living. So I was getting fed.

But I still wanted more. So much of what I was learning pointed back to the Word of God, but I wasn't able to use it as my primary source.

Well, it was about that time I heard about something offered to the women at my church—a Titus 2 ministry. I had no earthly idea who Titus was or what his second chapter said (at the time it would've taken me awhile to even find that book), but I was told the ministry focused on women and provided generational opportunities for older women to mentor younger ones. It sounded perfect.

That's it! I decided. I wasn't sure how I'd fit in, in terms of the younger generation—I was older than many of them— but I felt certain the mentors would be able to teach me something. So I signed up on the spot, was assigned to a group, and grabbed my Bible. I was ready to go!

I have to laugh when I think back to how it must have seemed to the other ladies that first night. Here I came marching in, a shiny new Bible tucked under my arm. I was nervous but determined. I plunked myself down and took a breath.

"Okay," I said. "I'll confess this is the first time that I've ever done this. Been in a small group, I mean. A Bible study." I grabbed my Bible and waved it in front of me. "I was supposed to bring this, right?"

Those dear ladies could've laughed at me. They could have looked down their noses at me and decided I wasn't really worth their time. They could have decided I was one of those people, one of the pitiful untaught who'd fumble around with her Bible, not even knowing where to find the book of Titus, looking lost while everyone else nodded in understanding of the night's lesson.

But that's not what they did at all. They practically crowed with delight as they surrounded me and welcomed me and asked me about my backstory. And when they heard it, and that I was a new Christian, they gave me their loving acceptance. They were excited to have me there and honored to be a part of my faith journey. In the months to come they took me under their wings and passionately set about teaching me through the Word and through their deeds. They were the living example of God's love for me, wonderful mentors and friends. And they were exactly what I'd needed and wanted all along.

I had a lot to learn. But I was up for the challenge. I absolutely drank in all the stories from the Bible, all the lessons our leaders gave. They recounted tales of the biblical greats—all those things I'm sure many of you learned on your mother's knee. Noah . . . Jonah . . . Peter . . . Paul . . . the parables Jesus gave to express His love and guidance . . . I ate them up like ice cream. My Bible was soon filled with notes and highlighted places and bookmarks. (And is there anything so beautiful as a well-used Bible?)

I was not only immersed in the Word under the guidance of my mentors but constantly seeking out other ways to learn. I asked for Bible studies to work on at home, books to read, things to look up. I had a driving passion to catch up to where I should've been all along. One of the reasons for my determination—the most important one, really—was so that I could teach my own children about the Bible and about Christ. I didn't want them to have the life I had, to miss out on all those years of fellowship and the warmth of God's love. So I took everything I was taught and fed it to my kids.

One of the best parts of being in a small group setting was that I had access to the knowledge of not only my mentors but also my peers in the group. They were all a bit ahead of me in their studies—it would've been just about impossible to find someone as unlearned as I was—so they, too, were able to mentor and teach me. In many ways I imagine it was a blessing to them to practice what they'd been recently taught, to find themselves in the teacher role rather than the student. They never minded all the times I pestered them for explanations and information and asked, "Where do I look to find out about this?" Or, "Who said that?" At times they even went out of their way to bring me studies or pass along scriptures they knew I would like or would benefit from.

Even between meetings I would be in touch with all the women. At church, of course. But also texting them, calling, e-mailing, Facebooking. Modern technology was my friend as I continued to glean everything I could from them. I did quite a bit of searching for materials online and brought them to the ladies to look over and talk with me about.

Our Titus 2 groups are amazing in how they're structured and what they do. The entire concept is such a blessing, to the younger women especially. The practical lessons, the life lessons, the spiritual lessons. The sense that they're being covered in prayer and nurtured by the mentors. Even all the fun moments and the food—it's all something to look forward to.

Likewise, I'm grateful for the friendships and relationships that are created and fostered. We hear it often, but through small groups, I've interacted with many women I might never have met. And I've been blessed by them and taught by them. I've made friends I know I'll have for life.

But the most important aspect of our small group to me personally has been the mentors' desire that their young women be immersed in the Word, that they would use their Bibles not only for Sunday-morning scriptures but as a living, breathing representation of God's presence in their lives. They have a lot of years of wisdom under their belts, so they know how important that is. They want us to understand how the Good Book contains the entire story of Jesus from start to finish, and to see the promise of all He desires and plans for us until we see Him again.

And I'm getting it. With their help, I'm taking it all in. I've been on a crash course in Bible 101!

One thing that's helped, I believe, is my absolute lack of embarrassment in admitting that I don't know something—or didn't know. Everyone knows I'm not going to shy away from that. Perhaps it's that I came to my faith later in life than many and therefore know how precious time is, but I decided early on that I wasn't going to be bashful about where I was, how little I knew, and how far I needed to go. "The word of God is alive and active," says Hebrews 4:12 (I know where that is now—I've got that verse highlighted). I want to be alive and active in my faith as well.

I think that's been a benefit to me in the long run. When you've nowhere to go but up and you open yourself wide, you can't help but be filled. That's all that's mattered to me—doing whatever I can to learn more about the God who saved me. And again, with my children's spiritual lives on the line, I'm not going to beat around the bush.

I came to that first Titus 2 meeting completely unaware of how deep and rich my spiritual life would become through Bible study. But those women patiently fostered my desire to learn, leading me by the hand as I grew in understanding. In a way, I guess it could be compared to the famous scene in Helen Keller's life when Annie Sullivan finally gets through to her at the water pump, opening Helen's mental eyes to the world around her. Just as Helen raced from object to object, ecstatically asking about it, I feel like I've raced from place to place in the Bible, drinking in God's Word, happy to finally understand it.

It's been an amazing journey. And I'm glad to be onboard.

If you ask the other women in Connie's Titus 2 ministry who their favorite sister in Christ is, many of them will say Connie. Not because they love her any more than they do the other ladies in their group. But because there's something precious about Connie and about her driving desire to grow in faith. She is an inspiration to many who have watched her transform before their eyes and grow in understanding.

And her joy is infectious. Through her enthusiasm, she has empowered many of her peers to be more comfortable talking about God, about their personal faith, about the Bible. Many of them might not have been quite so open if they hadn't had Connie forging a path for them. But her no-holds-barred approach has spread among each group she's been a part of. Because of her, the younger women are more transparent regarding their own feelings, more free with expressing themselves. And more willing to pick up their Bibles and explore God's Word. Her enthusiasm for what's on those pages piques the girls' interest.

Too, for many of the more seasoned ladies, she has brought a breath of fresh air to their own faith and desire for Bible study. There's something exhilarating about seeing God through the eyes of someone inexperienced in the Christian faith. As Connie said, perhaps there is a bit of Helen Keller excitement that adds a shine to the Bible stories and lessons we've heard throughout our lives. It's not that we don't love and appreciate the lessons, but when you've been in the church for so many years, they may become more commonplace than you want them to be. People like Connie—especially when they're coming to us for answers and asking us to look at Scripture with them—force us to dust off our feelings and thoughts about faith and biblical examples and examine them in different ways. There's something raw and open about those people that challenges us.

Imagine if Connie had not had a Titus 2 group to connect with. What might be different?

Well, first, let's look at Connie. There is no doubt that in terms of her faith and her understanding of the Bible, being a part of her small group catapulted Connie far beyond where she might have gotten to on her own, at least in that amount of time. Through the ministry and the mentoring of the others in her group, she was able to accelerate her learning. She had a one-stop shopping experience when it came to the base of biblical knowledge brought to the table. The collected wisdom of all the women there functioned as a sort of library for her, and she could pick and choose and check out information on many topics, such as what to do in certain situations and how to handle others. The women were ready and willing to provide answers to her needs.

She also had the benefit of their suggestions—books to explore, lessons to study, devotions to read. Again, picture it like a library staffer asking questions and then leading you to the perfect materials you need. She had her own personal reference librarian!

And Connie absolutely took advantage of that. As she said, she picked and prodded and asked and begged for every scrap she could gather. No one and nothing was off-limits. No one had any desire to set any boundaries for her—she had unfettered access to everyone, and they were blessed to see how she grew spiritually. And grow she did, in leaps and bounds.

Now, if Connie had not had those mentors and peers, where would she be? With her enthusiasm, I'm sure she'd be forging along, learning what she could. She'd be reading and highlighting and studying her Bible. She would probably have figured out where all the books of the Bible are. But without the guidance of the women in her group, she likely would be learning alone, without their insights to focus her on her specific needs. And she'd likely be behind where she is now in terms of knowledge.

And she might have been led astray in her learning. Too many times I have seen new Christians begin their study of Scripture with enthusiasm and a drive to learn. But along the way they hit roadblocks. Perhaps it's misinformation that leads them astray—a very real danger these days, especially with the availability of questionable materials on the Internet—and they have no one to gently guide them back to the truth. Perhaps it is a lagging of excitement because there's no one to keep pushing them forward, so they slowly stop digging in the Word until their Bible becomes just one of the many books stacked on the table. Whatever the case, there's a danger in studying the Word of God without godly wisdom backing you up every step of the way. Studying in isolation increases that danger.

So in that way, Connie's Titus 2 group was invaluable to her. As she said, she has a goal of training up her children in the Lord, and they are not young kids. So for her, time has always been of the essence, as well as making sure she kept to a God-ordained path of knowledge. What a blessing that she did have the resource of her small groups.

The other side of the picture is where Connie's small groups and peers might be if she'd never joined them. Again, I have no doubt that they would have remained vibrant and nurturing circles for all the ladies involved. But as I mentioned, there is also no doubt that Connie is a fire that makes everyone burn brighter. She has inspired others to grow in their own faith, pushed them to take steps they might not have, especially related to Bible study. So I know her presence has enriched the lives of many of the ladies in ways that would be missing if they hadn't had the opportunity to know her.

All these things are benefits of a Titus 2 ministry that I cannot stress enough. There is something powerful about the way small group mentoring pushes women to excel, to become better versions of themselves than they might have been on their own. The combination of nurturing and wisdom from the older generation, coupled with the support and friendship of the younger generation, creates an atmosphere of inspiration. Just as a coach motivates an athlete to perform ever better, a Titus 2 ministry gathers women and encourages them to do and be more.

Yes, there are other aspects to the ministry—many other lessons, as you've seen and will see here in this book. But not the least of them is the desire that all the women in the group grow and learn not just emotionally, not just relationally but spiritually through the Word. In some ways it is the base upon which all the rest is built.

The Bible is filled with verses about building your faith upon knowledge:

- "Choose my instruction instead of silver, knowledge rather than choice gold" (Proverbs 8:10).

- "For this reason, since the day we heard about you, we have not stopped praying for you. We continually ask God to fill you with the knowledge of his will through all the wisdom and understanding that the Spirit gives" (Colossians 1:9).
- "Who is wise and understanding among you? Let them show it by their good life, by deeds done in the humility that comes from wisdom" (James 3:13).
- "Wisdom is a shelter as money is a shelter, but the advantage of knowledge is this: Wisdom preserves those who have it" (Ecclesiastes 7:12).
- "For this very reason, make every effort to add to your faith goodness; and to goodness, knowledge" (2 Peter 1:5).

I could go on and on. But the point is that faith is linked to godly knowledge, and the study of the Bible is a crucial element in gathering that knowledge. We need to intentionally foster it not just in individuals but in a group setting. The combined insights of the many lead to discussions and a dissecting of the Word that enhances our understanding in ways we won't find in isolation. We need to encourage each other in our study of the Bible, pushing each other to do more, serving as catalysts and coaches on the journey.

Connie mentioned how beautiful a well-used Bible is, filled with colorful highlights and tagged pages and notes—all the personal touches that indicate an owner dedicated to learning more about God through His Word. My hope for you, my friend, is that you are either already on this journey or ready to seek out those who will mentor you in Bible study. I promise you will be enriched.

Heart Check

All Scripture is God-breathed and is useful for
teaching, rebuking, correcting and training in
righteousness, so that the servant of God may be
thoroughly equipped for every good work.

—2 Timothy 3:16–17

Be honest: do you study your Bible the way you know
you should? Explain.

_____

_____

_____

_____

How do you feel Bible study enhances your personal faith
walk? What are your favorite verses or stories? Why are
they your favorites?

_____

_____

_____

_____

What would it mean to you to supplement your Bible study with the shared knowledge of wise mentors and encouraging peers? Explain.

_____

_____

_____

_____

Lord, You command that we study Your Word as a way to know Your will. You have given us the entire story of the universe within its pages. Push me to immerse myself in the Bible and to find women who will encourage me to keep my feet firmly headed down that path.

When I first started coming to my Titus 2 small group, I'd never read the Bible. I didn't even own one. But they encouraged Bible study, so I finally bought one and started looking through it. I was fascinated . . . but a bit alarmed too. I kept thinking, *What is this? What am I supposed to do with it?* I didn't know how to read it, and even if I could, I wouldn't really have understood what it said. I was frustrated because I wanted so much to be able to use my Bible in my studies and to see on paper the things I'd heard about. But it was just too intimidating for me.

Well, God had His own timing because it all worked out. The first thing was that my mentors said to set aside the Bible I had and to go buy a children's Bible.

Okay, I thought, *it's a bit embarrassing to know I'm at a kid's level with all this.* But I had faith in my mentors, so I went to the store and bought what they said. And I read that thing in two days! I couldn't put it down. I was insanely happy to finally be able to read the stories I'd heard about and understand what they were about. I still have that Bible, and I still read it, especially to my kids.

But I've also begun to read my adult Bible as well. After having heard a lot of sermons, I understand more now. So when I read, it makes a lot more sense.

One of my friends and I started doing a Bible study on Saturday mornings. She uses a *Life Application Study Bible,* and I'd been eyeing them because I knew it would help me. But they're so expensive, and I decided I couldn't afford it.

My friend said, "Well, I have an extra one you can have." And she gave it to me!

I was so excited. The first thing I did when I got home that day was sit down and open it up without looking. And it opened to Proverbs 31. The perfect place. I read those verses like I never had before. And I saw all the explanations at the bottom and read those as well. And I was like, "Okay! I get it! I finally get it!"

So I just kept going. I'm still going. Every night I read until I can't keep my eyes open. One night not too long ago my four-year-old son was watching me read and make notes. He got so excited because I'd never written in a Bible before. I used to think I didn't want to mess it up, but now I want to write down my notes.

My son said, "I want to highlight it for you, Mom. You read and tell me what you want highlighted and I'll do it."

So that's what we do, every night. He comes in and I'll read and he highlights and we do it together. I'll say, "Oh, that's a good one—highlight that." And he does it for me. That is such an incredible blessing to me, to be studying the Word right there with my son, knowing that even at his young age, he's beginning to learn just how important it is in our lives.

I am so thankful for my Titus 2 group's focus on the Bible and how they've encouraged me in my studies. I feel like God is talking directly to me through that Bible. And I can't wait to listen to Him more!

—MARANDA, MENTEE

Small groups are good for women. They make women feel more comfortable about sharing their lives and hearts. Larger groups hinder that—you tend to sit back and listen and maybe not feel as much a part of things. And in large groups, some women tend to get lost in the numbers. You're just not as connected.

A Titus 2 small-group model takes care of that. It fosters such a sense of intimacy. You truly do know each and every woman sitting around the table or across the living room from you. Friendships are formed, tears are shed, and laughter is shared. Blessings are given and received between mentors and mentees, older women and younger. For those young women who need extra attention, the mentors can acknowledge that and spend extra time with them in prayer and pampering. I know I myself have experienced this situation with my girls on more than one occasion.

One of the greatest gifts I think Titus 2 groups offer is the chance to deeply study the Scriptures together. This is not to say our small groups are only Bible study gatherings—we do a lot more than that! But we do stress the need for devotion and study time. Exploring God's Word allows our young ladies an opportunity to learn together, discuss together, and gain encouragement together from what they read. It makes it more impactful, I believe. And I trust that it gives them an extra push to open the Bible on their own and see what God has to say to them for whatever they may need at that time. I know some of the girls already do—one woman calls her Bible time her "Middle of the Week Word from God." How wonderful that she sees her Bible that way and actively plans study time for herself. That might not have happened if she hadn't been a part of Titus 2.

Our intentional study of Scripture has at many times given women an opportunity to bring up particular issues they're struggling with that relate to what we're reading. They feel comfortable sharing, knowing what they reveal will be received in confidence. And everyone can look together for the answers the Bible may hold for that problem or challenge. Our small groups also give women the chance to speak up about whatever topics they'd like to study. And it definitely gives them the chance to speak out in general. Many are shy enough or unsure enough about their biblical knowledge that they'd never say anything in a crowd, so they've tended to get left out of discussion. Here, they're not. They're engaging in the process. They might not understand everything, but they have a circle of friends who can help explain it or learn it with them.

I'm glad these ladies have an opportunity in our Titus 2 small group to fellowship together, study the Bible together, learn together, support each other. They're finding friends for life—not just friendships with the women in the group but a friendship with the Holy Spirit, who speaks to them through God's Word.

—LINDA, MENTOR

CHAPTER SIX

OPEN TO CHANGE

Are You Teachable and Reachable?

> Teachability is not so much about competence and mental capacity as it is about attitude. It is the desire to listen, learn, and apply. It is the hunger to discover and grow. It is the willingness to learn, unlearn, and relearn.
> —*John Maxwell*

MIRANDA'S STORY

When I first joined my Titus 2 group, I had just moved back to my hometown after being away for over ten years. My small group was a huge help as I adjusted to my return, because it was definitely a new experience coming back after so long.

I'd left with a picture of everything and everyone frozen in my mind, sort of like a DVD on Pause. I'd been a teenager with no frame of reference for the world other than this place of my childhood. All my relationships were as a youth; the adults I knew at the time were as far from where I was emotionally and mentally at the time as the two sides of the Grand Canyon. To me, we were like different species! They were "the grown-ups" who were friends with my parents, those people I called "Mr. and Mrs." To them I was "that young Miranda." I couldn't even begin to conceive of their thought processes. And I'm sure they would have said the same thing about mine.

Fast-forward to now, and suddenly I was coming back as an adult. I'd gone to college, joined the workforce, gotten married, and forged a life for myself. I'd experienced adult joys and heartaches. I in no way thought of myself as that young girl who'd left town. I wasn't her. She was from another lifetime.

Yet I sort of thought that way about the town and the people in it—I thought I'd be unpausing that DVD and stepping back into the picture with everything the same as when I left it. Taking up with the same circle of friends, calling my friends' parents "Mr. and Mrs."

That was not the case, of course. Just like it had with me, life had continued for everyone. The town had grown. People had come and gone and grown up or grown old. Many had had major life changes—marriages or kids, jobs or houses. The church was drastically different from when I left. I had to adjust my expectations in that regard. I had to take the DVD out and put it away and start over.

I think the biggest challenge I had was in my relationships with the people I'd returned to. Everything had been placed into a different context. When I left, my sphere of influence was with my high school peers. Now I was an adult, as were they. Many were married with jobs and kids. Not only that, but "the grown-ups" who had seemed so foreign to me were now my peers. The people I'd called "Mr. and Mrs." were suddenly Tom and Ann or Rick and Susan, and instead of asking me how school or sports was going, they were asking me about my family and inviting me to dinner or to sit with them at church. And they didn't seem quite so old to me as I'd thought (of course, back then I thought people in their late twenties were old!). I was coming to them more or less on the same level rather than child to elder.

On the other hand, the kids I'd babysat way back when during church services or date nights were now calling me "Mrs." and asking if I needed a babysitter.

My new life was definitely an adjustment—in a way, it was like some sort of *Freaky Friday* movie switcheroo with everybody confused as to who was who and how old they were. Very surreal for me. For everyone else, too, I'm sure, as they tried to reconcile the young girl they'd last seen with the wife and mother now standing in front of them.

Even my relationship with my family, and especially with my mom, went through an adjustment period. Yes, we'd seen a lot of each other over the years. We'd spent vacations together and connected for holidays and special occasions. But quick visits are very different from daily interaction. It's hard to get a sense of things when you're a guest in someone's home or busy with the events that brought you there in the first place.

And as a wife with my own household to run, I'd created my own routine and ways of doing things over the years. So even something as simple as how I cleaned house—or something as complex as how I approached my marriage or childrearing—was sometimes different from how my parents had done it when I was young. That's a normal transition, but it still takes getting used to. They had to realize I was capable of handling my own home, and I had to realize I could approach them as an equal to ask questions and discuss various aspects of my life. It's such a lightning-bolt moment to realize your parents aren't just your parents anymore but also your adult friends. It's comfortable in a new and different way. But still, it's a big change.

So there were adjustments. I had to step away from the past and approach my community in the here and now. My Titus 2 small group that first year, and in the years after, was a big help. Through the ministry I met young, married, working mothers such as myself—ladies I'd never been in the same circles with before and therefore might not have had the opportunity to know. Some of them were just a few years older than I was, with a bit more experience in the ins and outs of home and family life. They were a great resource for the challenges of new parenthood, and I absolutely took advantage of that. I went to them for many practical issues, such as how to potty-train my kids or how to get them to stay down for naps. I was comfortable sharing my personal struggles as well. My new friends were there to support me through all of it. And they helped me build my adult identity and got me plugged back into the church and community on a new level. One of those women is now my best friend and has been by my side ever since those days.

On the other side of the coin were my budding relationships with those women older than I was—my Titus 2 mentors who had been married twenty, thirty, forty-plus years. What an amazing collection of women and wisdom they were! Once I got over my surprise at finding myself friends with a totally different generation (or two), I jumped in and ran with it. It was fun to develop new relationships with old acquaintances. It was fulfilling to have meaningful interactions with other age groups and to learn from them important life lessons. They taught me about how to be a godly woman, a Christian wife, and a mom. And yes, they corroborated many of the things I'd been taught by my own mom—an incredible mother and Titus 2 mentor herself. (Don't all daughters have to hear their mom's lessons coming out of someone else's mouth before they really believe them?)

Also, I was eager to go to these mentors regarding my spiritual life. I'd been blessed to grow up in a strong Christian family, and I'd carried my faith with me all the years I'd been away. So it wasn't as though I was struggling to "find myself" or learn how to be a Christian. But because I'd been shown through example all my life that my marriage and family had to be built on a solid foundation, I wanted to be proactive, and having the opportunity to study the Word of God under these older and wiser women was a blessing. They were happy to instruct me, and I soaked up everything they could teach me. They exemplified everything Paul must have envisioned when he wrote those words in Titus 2.

Our mentors were hard at work with *all* us younger ladies in the small groups, supporting us and teaching us with lessons specifically geared toward our life situations. We were encouraged to spend time in the Word. The monthly lessons were always Scripture-based and revolved around themes such as being a friend of God, learning how to be a wife of noble character, and how to study Scripture in practical and useful ways. They taught us how to love and respect our husbands and how to keep a peaceful home. Most of all, through our many small group discussions, they encouraged us to support each other in keeping our marriages honorable to God and being the wives the Lord calls us to be. I learned so much from those incredible women who were willing to teach us younger wives what it takes to have a godly marriage.

One of the things that has amazed me—especially as someone returning to my hometown and reacquainting myself with other women my age who have similar lives—is the number of my peers who *don't* take advantage of relationships with older women. I honestly don't get it. There are girls and women who have an attitude of,

"Sorry, but you're old. We can't really connect with you." They aren't being mean about it; they just can't comprehend it. They're puzzled at the idea. I mean, everybody knows your friends are supposed to be your own age, right? Older people just aren't in the same place as we are, right?

"Yes!" I try to tell them. The whole point is that we *aren't* in the same place. As young women, we don't need answers to the things we already know—we need answers to the things we *don't* know but those other women do! We *want* our mentors to be in a different place from us. That's what gives us the different perspective we need.

It's crazy, because I see a lot of younger women struggling in their lives—dealing with issues about marriage or school or relationships or parenting. And here is this amazing resource right in front of them, but they can't see it. They're trying to handle things themselves, or with a few friends in the same boat as they are. That's great for commiserating, but it might not always offer concrete and useful suggestions and options. They're all sinking in that same boat.

It's disappointing, because I want my peers to experience the same wise counsel I am. So I try whenever I can to help connect these different generations. I have a lot of conversations that end with, "Well, you should really talk to so-and-so about this." Sometimes they listen to me; sometimes they don't. But the ones who listen—aha, they get it! And it is awesome to see how they click with their new mentors and start to reap the benefits I've been enjoying. How could they not, when it's so easy?

I cannot endorse enough the whole concept of Titus 2 groups. Whether you grew up in a home that gave you spiritual guidance or one that didn't—whether you had a mom who taught you how to cook, clean, and raise your babies, or whether you had a mother who wasn't involved in your life at all—this ministry is like having multiple spiritual moms who will love you like a daughter and who will teach you alongside some of the best friends you'll ever make. You'll gain a tremendous amount of knowledge from them. You'll be fed, you'll be taught, and you'll be encouraged. You'll laugh, you'll cry, and you'll walk away at the end of each year a better wife, a better mother, a better daughter or sister. And ultimately a better person from when you started.

I know I am.

Teachable and reachable is a phrase we use a lot in our local Titus 2 women's mentoring ministry. It means a couple of different things. First, it asks that you be open to the instruction of your mentors and avail yourself of their knowledge and wisdom. That you be willing to listen to and accept and make use of their guidance. Second, it conveys the attitude of being approachable on a relational level. And not only that, but to *seek out* relationships with others. These are crucial qualities in a successful mentoring experience. We want our young ladies to be actively seeking not only the Lord but also interactions with others who can help them grow in their faith. Without the ability to be teachable and reachable, it's pretty much guaranteed you won't get very far. Or at least not as successfully as you might have. (It's one thing to cross the finish line and another to cross it first!)

Miranda is the perfect example of a teachable and reachable woman. As she said, she grew up in a Christian home. So she thankfully had a solid base on which to grow her faith. There were no glaring emotional needs in her background, no traumas or dysfunction such as what we've seen in some of the other stories in this book. That said, returning home after a long period away presented a unique challenge for her. She could have simply settled into her life and started up right where she left off, taking a low-key approach and continuing to have the one-dimensional and immature relationships she'd had with people in high school. It would have been the easy choice, and although they might have been disappointed, no one would have said anything.

But Miranda made a different decision. She didn't want to be the girl she had been. She didn't want to stay in the same safe rut. As she said, she was no longer that young girl. So she actively worked to carve out a new identity for herself—to re-present herself in the eyes of the community she'd left. Not only that, but she chose to continue to grow in her faith so she could honor God in her marriage and family.

Having the benefit of a Titus 2 ministry was a perfect vehicle for her. She eagerly sought and took advantage of her generational mentors, asking questions, calling or e-mailing them for advice, studying the books and scriptures they gave her. At meetings, she encouraged discussions that helped facilitate her desires—and the desires of others around the table with similar home and family situations. She wanted to know how to be the best wife, how to manage home and work, how to raise her kids the way her mentors had. She saw their successes, and she was smart enough to know that if she wanted the same experiences, she needed to go right to the source. So she did, without hesitation. She had just the right spirit that enabled her to be ministered to through a small group setting.

So Miranda is a teachable young woman with a hunger and thirst for knowledge and spiritual growth. She is also very reachable as an approachable, gentle soul with a sweet spirit. "I'm an open book," she said. "I want everybody to know who I am and where I'm coming from. Why waste time on hiding anything? It serves no purpose other than wasting emotional energy."

In part it has been that vulnerability that has allowed Miranda to forge instant and strong relationships, not only with older generations but also with her peers. As she said, she has made it her mission to approach struggling young women and connect them with the mentors she knows can help them. She wants to foster teachability and reachability in those girls. For that reason, Miranda is often the go-to gal assigned to help out at church when new young women come to join. Everyone knows she'll take care of them and help them get started on the right track.

Miranda and her husband, Ryan, have also spent the past few years working at a yearly marriage retreat. Having a teachable and reachable spirit is crucial to a marriage, and many couples have benefited from the lessons Miranda and Ryan have taught. This past year they became leaders in charge of part of the whole program. This is partly due to their openness and willingness to share their experiences with others. But it's also another example of how Miranda's desire to connect and listen and learn has enriched her life.

She herself would tell you she never expected to be in the position she ended up in. "I never thought I had any leadership skills," she said. "I absolutely never even dreamed that was possible, that someone would want me to be in charge of something like this, something so important."

Perhaps that was true at one time. But having spent the past few years deliberately placing herself in situations where she could grow and learn from her mentors strengthened the innate skills she did have. Watching as her elders efficiently got the job done taught her how to do the job as well. And forming relationships with those who were in charge of the marriage retreat allowed those leaders to know Miranda on a more intimate level and see that she and Ryan were ready for a position of responsibility.

That was a huge lightbulb moment for Miranda. She was seeing a direct result of the years she'd put into presenting a teachable attitude. She'd just never thought ahead far enough to realize that one day, as a result of her humble and teachable attitude in the marriage retreat, she'd be asked to step in and take over, like a runner passing a baton.

I wonder sometimes where Miranda would be on her faith journey if she hadn't returned to her hometown and joined the local Titus 2 ministry. Or where she'd be spiritually if she'd come home and just slipped back into her old life without joining a small group. To be honest, I can't picture it, because she is so driven to grow that I can't imagine her doing anything other than making the opportunities happen. She would be teachable and reachable no matter where she was. I know her mentors and peers are glad she ended up where she did, though, because she has inspired many of them to grow as well.

And again, that inspiration was facilitated by her small groups, where a roomful of women influenced one another in positive ways. I can't stress enough that a Titus 2 ministry is not made up of isolated events or people but a community of believers consistently encouraging each other to grow and lead happy and successful lives.

My friend, I encourage you to find a similar community of believers. I pray that you are teachable, that you are filled with the kind of fire that desires knowledge of God and propels you toward those who can fill that need. And I pray that you are reachable, that you listen to and hear God in the voices of the wise mentors around you—and that you encourage others to do the same.

Heart Check

When I was a child, I talked like a child, I
thought like a child, I reasoned like a child.
When I became a [wo]man, I put the ways of
childhood behind me. For now we see only a
reflection as in a mirror; then we shall see face
to face. Now I know in part; then I shall know
fully, even as I am fully known.

—1 Corinthians 13:11–12

What do you believe are the attributes of a teachable
woman? Do you consider yourself to be teachable?
Explain.

_____

_____

_____

_____

Likewise, what do you feel best exemplifies the heart of a
reachable woman? Do you consider yourself reachable?
Explain.

_____

_____

_____

_____

List at least one way you will work to foster a more teachable and reachable attitude in yourself. Then jot down a few names of those you will reach out to in order to help you grow in your faith.

_____

_____

_____

_____

Lord, of all the many aspects of a godly woman, I know being teachable and reachable are two of the most important. Give me the desire to learn from those around me and the heart to be open to what they say. I want to grow closer to You in every way I can.

There is a lot to be said for learning from other people's mistakes. There is also a whole lot to be said for learning from other people's successes. If we fail to recognize and take the opportunity to learn from others' life lessons—the good and the bad, the pretty and the ugly—then we are missing out on a tremendous life education. Often, getting the opportunity to foster such interactions is the hardest part. That's where a Titus 2 ministry steps in. It has created a place for us youngsters to learn from the "seasoned" women who have made mistakes and had many successes.

Titus 2 mentors create an environment in which to learn from and grow with one another. In this environment, the more experienced women are eager and willing to share their stories and life experiences. They want to help us younger women as we drag our bodies through the trenches of young motherhood and young marriages. They're there to provide support—emotional, spiritual, mental. Sometimes even physical as they help with chores or babysitting.

As beneficial as that is, we as the younger women still have the job of listening to and being receptive to the advice and wisdom offered by our mentors. Words of wisdom mean very little if they are not received and applied. And what a waste that would be to let them slip through our fingers.

In my few years of participating in my small groups, I have learned that you take away as much as you allow yourself. The majority of the time I leave completely filled to the brim with new ideas and inspiration for loving my husband, caring for my family, and serving the Lord. There have been times, however, when I have left a group at the end of a year and realized I have gleaned very little.

But you know what? I am responsible for that. It's nobody's fault but my own if I didn't actively seek to connect and make sure I was taking something home each month to work on. The times in which I have left empty or unfulfilled were not because I was not being fed, but because I did not eat. (And yes, we do also eat some delicious food!)

I'll admit I have not always been receptive to others' instruction and mentoring. Pride and I have quite a history together. Growing up, I was not always eager to hear my mother's advice or instruction. (I know—hard to believe a daughter won't listen to her mother, right?) Thankfully, God has done a fair amount of work on me, and I have realized the value of sitting at the feet of those who have gone before me. I know they love me and want to help guide my steps—and now, as a wife and mother of young ones, I crave that guidance!

Our Titus 2 ministry has taken on the job of identifying and creating an opportunity for us to learn from others who have been there and done that. Yet it is our job to grab a strong hold on that opportunity and soak up what we can. God created us to be relational, and I believe that with all that I am. We cannot waste a single opportunity to utilize our relationships to learn how to create a better life. To be a better wife, a better friend, a better mother. And to do it all to the glory of Him!

—KATELYN, MENTEE

When I was asked for some remarks regarding mentoring, I thought back to the time when I was a young mom with five small children, a husband in school, a very limited budget, and a mother who lived two thousand miles away. Oh my, those days were difficult for me as I tried to figure out the ins and outs of running my own household without the benefit of any close friends or relatives to see me through. There were many days I longed for counsel—on everything from whether a child was sick enough to go to the doctor to how to cut up a chicken. But I really didn't have anyone local I could go to. So I was forced to muddle through on my own. Thankfully, everything turned out okay, but it was definitely a lot harder than it had to be.

The same is true even today—has been true for all of recorded history. Rearing children and managing a home on our own by the seat of our pants is never ideal and almost always brings about stress and uncertainty. This stress spills over into our marriages, which brings problems of its own. Yet rather than seek out help, we often withdraw in our misery, trying to handle the situation on our own so we don't have to admit we're struggling. So our families struggle along with us and the issue snowballs.

It doesn't have to be that way!

In the years since we began our Titus 2 ministry, I have been associated with many women—everyone from young mothers just beginning their families to moms of teenagers to empty nesters with kids in college. But rather than exist in isolation, all these women consciously and intentionally work to foster relationships and help each other. They are always open and eager to share a story about a particular concern and are earnestly looking for answers from their friends. And they're finding those answers, as others in the group seek to encourage those around them. It is a constant cycle of giving and taking, teaching and learning.

For me, it has been a privilege to share and respond to the needs of my young women within the security of a loving home environment. We have laughed and cried and prayed together as thoughts, experiences, and ideas flowed among members of the group. And I've seen the results in the confidence and caring of the ladies around me, and how that then spills out into the church community. Joining generations together in a congregation has a profound effect on the way the different ages view each other. Older women are involved in learning more about young families and their lives instead of criticizing them for letting their children run through the building. Young women no longer slide past elders with a polite "Excuse me," but stop for a hug and a sweet exchange.

This is happening in our church, and it's a change that would not have taken place on its own. It's happening because of Titus 2. One of my daughters works with teenagers and has often said that you have to force them to have fun by having a plan and organizing games. The same concept can be applied to all ages. We are very comfortable with the status quo unless prodded to move out of it. Titus 2 small groups do exactly that, moving us out of our seats and into the lives of other women where we can all learn from each other.

And it works—every single time.

—JO, MENTOR

CHAPTER SEVEN

OPEN TO GOD

The Blessings of Spiritual Maturity

How you respond to what is happening in your life can make a difference. Your conduct in the confusion, your resolve while enduring pain and your positive thought process during the tribulation can help you handle what is happening in your life. Those are . . . moments that make the difference as you are maneuvering the waves of life. Those moments are filled with the presence of God and how you respond and behave in those moments makes all of the difference.

—*Dr. Glen A. Staples*

TIFFANY'S STORY

I grew up going to church, so I always knew about God and having a relationship with Jesus. Although in hindsight I should point out that I knew *about* God and *about* a relationship with Jesus, not that I actually *made* those connections on a personal level. Still, I had godly parents who worked hard to model their faith and instill biblical values in my siblings and me. We went to services every week, and I was a part of our youth group.

So it was really only my own ignorance that led me away from a God-centered life. Yes, I still believed in Him. But I certainly didn't live as though I was His. My husband and I made some bad choices, put ourselves in the center, and lived a worldly lifestyle for many years. We felt good about things, felt we were living the life we wanted. We were successful. We had a home. Jobs. I had our first child. Life was going well.

Or was it? If I had ever really stopped to take stock of things during that time—listened to my inner heart— I would have admitted that, no, things were not as on track as they seemed. We were placing our priority on the wrong things. We continued to make bad choices that affected us and our family. I was not fulfilled, no matter how I tried to act like I was. And neither was my husband. We spent our time searching for something we couldn't put our finger on, something that would bring real meaning to our lives and put things in perspective. And although things were okay overall and my husband and I loved each other very much—and still do—there were cracks in our marriage that nothing we did could fill.

I personally felt I was just going through the motions. I wanted more than I had—more than the day-to-day life I lived, the things I bought, the people I knew. Again, if I'd really stopped and taken stock, I would've admitted I knew exactly what was missing. There was a God-shaped hole in the center of my life that nothing else was going to fill. But for a time I simply wasn't ready to admit that.

Thankfully, due not only to my family and friends standing in the gap for my husband and me, but also the Holy Spirit relentlessly pursuing us, I recommitted my life to God several years ago. And as you might expect, everything came very suddenly into perfect clarity. I knew exactly where I'd been, the mistakes I'd been ignoring, and where I needed to be. I was so thankful to have a focus, so glad to let go of all the rest and embrace the One who fulfilled me. It was a relief to know I had purpose and know I was loved by a God who saw past my silly, ridiculous attempts to control my destiny and told me, *I have you now. You're Mine.*

He did and I am. I closed the door on the old me and I haven't looked back.

Please understand: it hasn't been easy. It's no simple thing to unhook yourself from a life that revolves around the things of the world. But God has been patient with me, and I've steadily worked to center myself on Him. My friends would agree I'm pretty passionate about that!

By far the most precious helpers on my journey have been my Titus 2 mentors and ladies. They have been a rock for me. A lighthouse. When I first came to them, I was a new Christian, so I needed a lot of guidance. I'm grateful I had such a resource as them to turn to. And they were up to the task. It's what they do! They probably didn't know at the outset how much of their time I would demand and all the questions and requests I would have, but they willingly met the challenge and have never let me down.

And I've been eating it up! Just racing through it all. Through the different groups the past few years, I have developed close relationships with women of all ages— women who all teach me in their own ways. I have my mentors, the leaders who facilitate the group interaction and the learning process for all us younger ones. But the other women in the group have been important to my faith as well. I've had a lot of catching up to do, so they all mentor me, give me advice on parenting and daily living, provide examples of how to be a loving wife. They encourage me. They support me.

It's funny—until joining my Titus 2 group, I had never really thought that I should be, or even needed to be, friends with women who are much older than I am. But that's where I found myself. And it was a blessing. One of my mentors is a woman considerably older than I am. I'm actually not even certain how old she is because she's one of those women who looks great for her age. But I do know for sure she has lived a lot more of life than I have! She has a huge family full of children and grandchildren and, I believe, great-grandchildren too.

What amazed me the most in getting to know her was how easy it was to be with her, talk with her, share my stories, and even relate to the ones she told me. I never thought I would have so much in common with someone who wasn't even close to my age. I never thought I'd call someone of her generation a close friend. But I do. And the wisdom I have received from her—both through teaching and in casual conversation—is something I find myself thinking about almost every day.

So I'd have to say the small group relationships that have meant the most to me in my journey have been those with the older ladies in my groups. I'm in my late twenties, but I've developed friendships with women in their thirties and older. Some, like I said, a lot older. And they're all women with the kind of experience and knowledge I want to have in my own life. I made a conscious decision to humble myself before them and learn from them. It wasn't always easy. I had to remind myself I didn't know it all. (I still don't. How could I? There's so much to learn!) My disregard for godly guidance—along with the immaturity that had made me think I had things in control—was what had gotten me into trouble before. I was determined to do things differently this time. To take advantage of the wealth of knowledge in front of me.

That's part of the whole point of a Titus 2 ministry, right? If I hadn't been open to learning, then it would have been nothing more than an exercise in social interaction. And I'd had plenty of that in the past. I wanted more.

So I sat there and laid out my heart to those women and asked for their guidance. And it's been a blessing. The maturity of the older women—both in their faith and in their lifestyles—has been an inspiration to me. I have grown so much because of them, come so much further than I was. My prayer life is richer because of them. My Bible study. My relationship with my church and friends.

I'm especially thankful for the growth in my relationship with my husband and my kids. I had another child during my early years in the ministry, and through my mentors' modeling of what godly mothering is and their gentle insistence that I look to God as the best model of all, I have learned to be the sort of parent my children need. For instance, I've realized how important it is to me that they know how to behave. Not just the usual "how to act in public" manners, but behaving as representatives of the body of Christ, even at their young age. My children represent us as a family. Being a part of my Titus 2 small groups and seeing all those women with their children, being in church regularly and going to Bible classes, placing my kids in their own classes, has given my husband and me the opportunity to see how other Christian parents do this thing called *family*. I feel that we as believers approach that concept differently than those outside the church—in a way that honors our commitment to God. I wanted to make sure I was teaching my own children the right way, right from the start.

My Titus 2 ladies have supported me with that 100 percent. No, not just supported, but lovingly demanded. They know how important it is. I'm not even sure how it's possible, but I feel like these women have deepened my love for my kids. I suppose it's that they constantly reaffirm the enormity of God's plan for them, for us, and how important it is to seek His guidance as I raise them. I see my kids more through His eyes because of my mentors.

My Titus 2 ladies have not only helped me with parenting, but they have nurtured me within every aspect of my life—my home life, work life, and spiritual life. They have been examples of where I need to be and what I need to be doing. I'm humbled by their care. In many ways their attention has motivated me. I feel like, if they are putting so much faith in me that they're pouring themselves into mentoring me, then I need to honor that with my commitment. It's to my own benefit!

So I've gone at it as hard and as faithfully as I can. I'm one of those ask-ask-ask people. I want to know everything! I'm forever grabbing friends and asking them to give me advice, show me what to do, point me toward the right book or resource, send me in the right direction. Just get me started and I'll run with it. I've learned very much in a short amount of time.

And I've taught my children what I've learned. That's something I'd never even considered before—teaching my children about the Bible and about God. I guess I thought that was only something that the preacher or the Bible class teachers at church were supposed to do. Or the vacation Bible schools I went to as a kid. But I have many Christian friends who have shared ideas with me about how they talk to their children about God or how they teach them praise songs and sing along with them in the car. I've even gotten suggestions for Bible storybooks to read to my children at bedtime. That has opened up a whole new world to us—not just for my children but also for me. I think I learn as much as my kids do when I read them Old Testament stories like Jonah or Samson or baby

Moses being sent down the river in a basket. I need those lessons as much—or perhaps more—than they do!

So yes, lessons such as those and others have been priceless to me. My children are young. I'm still a fairly young Christian. I work. So does my husband. Life is one challenge after another. But I want more than anything to be a godly mother, a godly wife, and a godly friend and church member. And through my Titus 2 group—with the help of both the younger ladies and the older ones—I have a ready resource for all the advice I could ever want, as well as a listening ear whenever I'm overwhelmed. I don't get that at work. I don't get that anywhere else but in small group. Nothing compares.

To be honest, I can't even list all the things I've learned from the women in my group, or how they have taught me to keep moving forward, to keep working to learn more. All I can say is my Titus 2 ministry came to me at exactly the best time in my life. It was just what I needed and everything I hoped it would be. And I can't wait to keep learning from everyone who's a part of it.

Tiffany is a great example of what happens when a motivated woman is willing to learn from her Titus 2 mentors. The growth in her spiritual maturity has been enormous. She's learned in leaps and bounds, far more and far more quickly than she might have on her own. She is a dear woman who inspires others with her radical love for God and her desire to continually mature in Him. She is open and eager to learn, and it shows. Not only in the way she has deepened her wisdom and understanding, but also in how she has developed strong relationships with the women around her who help her grow. The Titus 2 small group model was made for women like her. She has jumped in with both feet, and her mentors and friends would tell you it's been wonderful to see the transformation in her.

I believe one of the hallmarks of Tiffany's growth has been the enthusiasm she shows and her unfailing desire to develop in her relationship with God. She makes no bones about the fact that she is there to learn. She is unflinching in that purpose. And to her, knowledge isn't simply for knowledge's sake—what she learns, she wants to make use of in her life. So she turns right back around and funnels that information to her interactions with loved ones. She is dedicated to her family, and she knows that how she chooses to live her Christian life will greatly affect them. Aside from God, her husband and children are the most important things to her, front and center in her vision. So she's definitely motivated.

I liken it to those times when your doctor gives you a prescription for whatever ails you. He explains the benefits of the medicine, why you need it, and what it will do, and then hands you a square of paper with his scribbles all over it. And what does the doctor do next? He looks at you in all seriousness and says, "Make sure you get this filled, and take all of it."

Then it's up to you. You can take that prescription to the pharmacy and get it filled. You can pull the bottle out of that white paper bag it always comes in and hold it in your hand, knowing the medicine inside that container will make you well. But if you don't open the bottle and actually take the medicine inside, it's useless to you. If the pills stay in the bottle, it's nothing more than a noisy rattle and you're still sick. You cannot get well without making use of the resource given to you.

The same thing goes for the resources God places before you—if you don't use them, you're not going anywhere; you're just spinning your wheels. And Tiffany gets that. She realized that it wasn't enough simply to be a part of a church community, not enough simply to have faith. She needed to do something with those things. So she has devoted herself to growing and maturing in knowledge. She observes godly models around her, taking mental notes—and often written notes!—so she can go home and imitate their actions in her own life. She listens to the Bible studies and doesn't just pack her notes away until the next month, but she rereads them and finds ways to live out the suggestions. She asks for advice and then uses that advice rather than squandering it. She is proactive in her actions regarding a godly marriage and parenting—and in her decisions regarding her own faith walk. She is actively engaged in the process of growing and maturing in Christ.

I imagine Tiffany would have fit in well with the believers of the early church. We know they were enthusiastic. We know they pursued Jesus with all their hearts and sought to live lives that honored Him. They followed Him and then the apostles, wanting every day to learn more. What those early believers were hearing was such a radical change from everything they'd known before that they couldn't wait to experience it and actively pursue more of it. Peter said of those days, "Like newborn babies, crave pure spiritual milk, so that by it you may grow up in your salvation" (1 Peter 2:2). Tiffany is like that. She is longing. She is pursuing God. She is twisting off the cap to the medicine bottle and gulping it down.

Her mentors and peers have seen the results of that fire in her. She is transformed. She is wise beyond her years—very much so, to the point it's almost startling to realize she's still in her twenties. She is thoughtful and persistent in seeking to understand the Word of God. She digs deeper, studies more, discusses, explores. And she shares what she's learned. At times she is the teacher, as she brings to the ladies a perspective they haven't seen before or a book to recommend or a bit of information she's uncovered. Or takes what she's learned to others outside our small groups and ministers to them.

If there had not been a Titus 2 ministry for Tiffany, I honestly don't know where she'd be today in terms of her marriage, her parenting, and certainly her faith. I'm not sure where her transparency and openness would have led her, or if being plugged into a church home would have been enough. Tiffany needed a small group setting to foster her spiritual growth and to feel comfortable enough to share her hopes and desires. She needed the intentional direction of mentors who wisely guided her. And she insisted on taking what she learned and making it more.

It's these things in Tiffany's life that have allowed her to experience her spiritual maturation process. Her eagerness has made her learning progress faster than anyone would have expected, including herself. And it's exciting to think of what the future holds for her since she's come so far in so short a time.

Dear reader, I ask you to take a moment for self-reflection. Faith in God is paramount. But we are not to have a stagnant faith. God requires more of us. One of those requirements is making use of our faith to grow in discernment and spiritual maturity—a process we must actively foster in our lives. Where are you with that? Do you need help and encouragement, a boost? Then I hope you will seek out others to help you mature. It will lead to a more fulfilling life and a more intimate relationship with our God.

Heart Check

For this reason, since the day we heard about you, we have not stopped praying for you. We continually ask God to fill you with the knowledge of his will through all the wisdom and understanding that the Spirit gives, so that you may live a life worthy of the Lord and please him in every way: bearing fruit in every good work, growing in the knowledge of God.

—Colossians 1:9–10

Where would you put your spiritual maturity right now on a scale from 1 to 10, with 1 being "very immature" and 10 being "very mature"? Explain.

_____

_____

_____

_____

What are your thoughts on the idea of moving beyond a static faith to a continually maturing one? Do you feel you're on that path?

_____

_____

_____

_____

Who among your female friends or acquaintances do you feel could push you toward a more mature faith? Why is that?

_____

_____

_____

_____

Father, like any good dad, You desire for me to grow in knowledge and maturity, not because You find me lacking, but because You see the potential in me. Help me push myself forward and deepen my faith. Lead me to the women who can guide my efforts.

Being a part of a Titus 2 ministry has shown me that all women go through tough times. Sometimes, when I feel like no one understands my thoughts or feelings, it is very comforting to know that the women in my group—including my mentors—have gone through times just as hard, if not *harder*, than I have. And seeing how the older women cling to their faith during very difficult situations has given me a model for how I need to react in similar situations. These women don't give up; they pray and keep pushing through until they're on the other side. They let me know I can survive too. I am not alone. God is with me, and these ladies are with me as His representatives on earth. I've learned to be stronger than I might have been without them. That is a precious gift and something I know will serve me all my life.

One of the most rewarding parts of my time with these ladies has been having friends to talk to when days are tough and I feel like I'm being attacked from every angle—and we all know that happens a lot in today's world! But no matter how stressed I am or hurting or confused, there is always someone in my Titus 2 group who can help me work through my issue and give me perspective. They teach me and give me understanding and wisdom. Not only am I being comforted, but I'm learning from the experience. And I'm growing stronger because of it.

I love those times when someone will give me a Scripture verse or send me a text or give me a call right at the moment I need it most. I may not have even told anybody how I'm feeling, but somehow they just know and want to lift me up. That's been a blessing to me. I love that our mentors are so nurturing. And I'm inspired to know they're so in tune to hearing and feeling whatever the Holy Spirit is prompting in them.

That's something I really work toward in my own life—growing in spiritual maturity and discernment. Our mentors challenge all of us younger ladies with that, and they're great role models for what a Christian life looks like. They want to show us how important it is to live and breathe our faith so that we're open to God's prompt- ings and can minister to our friends and loved ones just as easily as they do to us. And they make it clear it's not something that comes naturally to every woman, not something we're just born with. We have to work at it and help it grow. It's something we cultivate in ourselves through godly instruction and through godly relation- ships. We're learning from their example, and then we're becoming examples for other women in the church and community. And for our families and children.

I'm working on it! And I'm seeing others around me working on it too. We're all in this together.

There are so many blessings that have come to me from my many seasons in our Titus 2 mentoring groups. I am thankful for the many friendships I've made and the laughter and tears shared, the comfort and support given by my friends and mentors alike. They've all helped me become the woman I am today, and I'm glad for their godly influence in my life.

—AMY, MENTEE

Our Titus 2 ministry at church has been a blessing to me and to all the women involved. Those of us who attend the small group meetings have cultivated a closer connection, and we've expanded our circle of intimate relationships. I never would have been able to meet and become so close to so many women if I hadn't been a part of the ministry. I'm sure it's the same with all the women involved.

Being a part of a Titus 2 group has made a big difference in getting to know women of all ages. Normally in our church, we would just get together with women from our own age groups. But through our small groups we have been able to bond with younger and older women. We have a large group of new mothers at our church, and it has been great getting to know them on a more personal level. I would have loved to have a program like this when I was a young mom! I know the ladies at our church are grateful for our support, both physically and spiritually.

It's so hard these days to get to know and connect with people at church. That's unfortunate, but it's a fact. Small groups are important because they provide a place where women feel safe enough to come together and talk about their personal problems and how to deal with them according to God's Word. They find others with whom they can pray and study and grow. Small groups provide a safe haven, which promotes relationships and growth. When we grow, we learn.

What's especially nice about a Titus 2 ministry is that within our groups we have Christian women of all ages and places in their lives. So we have a rich garden of knowledge for learning how to be a better wife, a better mother or sister or grandmother, a better friend. I'm always looking for good role models to help me grow as a Christian. And as a mentor myself, I consider it a privilege to guide the young women in my own group on their spiritual journey and to see them grow in faith and maturity as they become more comfortable with each other and open themselves up. I've really enjoyed having these women in my home to share a meal, Bible study, and friendship.

We have such a talented and God-loving group of women at our church, and we are blessed to have such a wonderful program as our Titus 2 ministry to bring us all closer to God and each other. I look forward to seeing how He continues to work in all our lives and especially the younger generation.

—JULIE, MENTOR

CHAPTER EIGHT

OPEN TO SHARING

Every Moment Is an Evangelism Moment

The hope that we have in Christ is so gloriously wonderful, why would we ever keep it to ourselves? When we refuse to communicate the Gospel there is nothing more cruel or selfish in all of humanity. Because we do believe that it is the only way—Christ is the only name—by which men and women can be saved. And to withhold that name and that news because it's difficult is on par with any other atrocious thing humanity has ever seen.

—*Britt Merrick*

KAY'S STORY

Well, my story begins a lot earlier than most women involved with our Titus 2 ministry. I've always had a heart for working with the younger generation. I think it began with seeing how my grandmother taught me. She was the epitome of evangelism without ever saying that's what she was doing. She simply lived and breathed it.

I loved my Nanny dearly. She probably never went to school past fourteen, so it's not like she had a big education with books. But she had an education in life. The lessons she taught weren't book, chapter, and verse at all. They were simple and direct, like "Pretty is as pretty does." And the Golden Rule. She talked about things like being faithful, being honest, making promises and keeping them. She spoke to me constantly about what the inner self should be. "You should be kind," she'd say. "You should be gentle," and so on. She named the fruit of the Spirit, but she never called them that. She lived it because she knew it was right, but she said it in her own words. And she took every opportunity to teach. We'd be shelling peas or shucking corn or swinging on the porch, and she would share things and we would talk about living right.

That was my life being raised by a godly grandmother. Not a godly mom, mind you. Not godly parents. My dad was a good man, but he wasn't a godly man. My mama had problems. She drank too much, smoked too much. Especially after my father died, she sort of went wild and didn't mother me the way a woman should. So my Nanny was the best thing in my life. I guarded in my heart all the things she taught me and the way she shared her faith.

It wasn't that I didn't make mistakes in life, though, because I did. I wasn't perfect, I'll tell you. I made some bad choices when I was younger that made for many rough years. But I could've been a much worse person. And as hard as it was, I could have had a much worse life. I know this is true.

Thankfully, God took the mistakes I made and the mistakes my husband, Phil, made and created something wonderful from them. I have an amazing life and a family I love dearly. They are living godly lives and making a difference in the world, and I am so grateful to God for that. More than that, because of my life experiences—the good and the bad—I have some important lessons I can teach other women. Because of my experiences, I'm excited to teach those lessons and tell my stories and hopefully make an impact in their lives. I'm happy to teach them not to make the mistakes I made. To teach them there is a God who loves them and wants good things for them.

I remember one night I was at a group meeting at another woman's house. We'd had our meal and our talk and had worked on the lesson for the night, and as sometimes happens, things ended a bit quicker than usual. And so we were all sitting around chatting when I felt something stir inside me. I told the ladies, "I feel like the Holy Spirit is telling me to do something right now."

They all looked at me like, *Okay, what's she going to say now?*

I said, "I know some of you here, but a lot of you I don't know. So I'm going to do something: I'm going to tell you my story. You know my recent history. But you don't know about the mistakes I made early on in life and the bad years I had with my husband."

And so I told them my story. There's a lot to it, but I tried to keep it to the mini version. And as I sat there talking, I saw one young girl I didn't know sitting by herself and listening to every word. She was so intent on me, and she had tears coming down her face, so I knew what I said was affecting her.

When I finished, I went over to see her. "Are you all right?" I said.

And she looked up at me and very simply answered, "I need to talk to you."

"Great," I said. "Let's talk."

And she said, "I don't know Jesus Christ as my Savior."

"Well then," I answered. "We do need to talk."

Over the following weeks I met with her. She explained that she was in a very bad place in her life and marriage and honestly didn't know what she was going to do. She'd reached absolute rock-bottom. So we counseled her and ministered to her and loved her back to a better place, and in the end I'm happy to say she became a Christian.

All of that—the transformation of a young and precious life—started with the moment I took a step in faith and shared my story. Think about what might have happened if I'd never had the strength to do that?

Now that's the power of small group mentoring. And it shows just how perfect a setting it is for sharing, for getting to the heart of things in a place where everyone is free to be themselves. At church you don't get to know people. You don't learn about them; you don't learn from them. Most times in church you're only there with people you know. You go in, you sit, you sing the hymns, you listen to the sermon. And it might be a great sermon. Don't get me wrong—I love church. But you don't meet people there.

And even if you did, you wouldn't think of sharing the real you, your inner secrets. It's all, "Hi, sister, how are you doing?" We pretend everything's okay, and that's a shame. Because until you break it down, you're not getting it out. That's what a Titus 2 group is for. It's a place where the older women teach the younger women and represent Christ to them and show them it's okay to let it all out.

I once had a woman in my group who shared that her family didn't know Jesus at all. She sat there in tears and talked about how she'd been going it alone. She'd thought about suicide because her life was so sad. Her family was not kind. They didn't know the Lord, and that rejection hurt her.

She broke down in front of us and said, "But here's the thing: this is my family, this group of ladies. You're the ladies I love. You're the ones who keep me accountable and teach me what the Word says and how to make it in life." With us she'd found a group of God's people who loved her, and it made all the difference in her world.

Another woman shared a different type of difficult situation. Her son was deep into drugs, so bad that one day the drug dealer himself called her up and said, "I've got your son. He's right here. You need to come get him." Imagine the heartache of getting that call.

Well, she went over there to collect her son. And while she was there, she got down on her knees and held both their hands and prayed to God for them. When she got through, both the son and drug dealer were crying. And to both of them she said, "This is no life for you. You do not have to live like this." The drug dealer said, "Lady, I might quit. This is the most touching thing. I've never felt anything like this."

Now, we may never know what that dealer did or if he made a change. But this woman's son is now in a rehab program. And that is because she had the strength to speak God's word to them, to reach out no matter how scary or painful, because those lives were worth it. Not only that, but she was able to share her story to us ladies in her small group. Why? Because she felt comfortable enough to do so. She said to us, "I knew I could tell you. No matter what."

Many women in my group struggle with problems at home—some terrible. You know who's right by their side every step of the way? Their group. Right there. These women know they can call somebody and say, "I need you," and that friend will be there. That closeness and that camaraderie and accountability and that love just spill out and carry these women.

And again, it's being in a home, being in an intimate place where the conversation can get personal. That's the best scenario for telling people about God, for showing women how God lives and works in your life. You're right there, in the moment, being real.

You've heard it already, but I'll say it again—it doesn't matter what your house looks like. I'm not the best housekeeper, and maybe you're not either, but the thing is the women don't look at that. They look at you. They feel your warmth, your welcoming attitude; they smell the food you cook for them. That's what matters. Not how your house looks. So many women choose not to open up their homes to others. They may be ashamed of it or the people in it. They may say they're too poor. Well, so was I, for years! My husband was a commercial fisherman—try living with that smell for years!

The women in my group came in one day and I'd burned the dinner. I was saying, "I'm so sorry" and running around scraping the tops off the rolls and throwing away things! But I kept going. I never dreamed of turning them away. They saw me in a crisis, but they didn't see me come unglued. Instead, we laughed.

That's life. You open your home. You practice hospitality; you reach out to women. That's what you do, because that's all that matters—taking an opportunity to show God to someone. Talking to them. Sharing. I teach my ladies to do the same. You might be scared or nervous. And when you first start sharing your story, you might only be able to do or say so much. You might think, *I can't expose that. I can't tell them that.* But I teach them that when they share, they're helping someone. You may not see it in the moment, but someone's listening. You're always making a difference. So you should never worry about the *how* or the *what.* Be real, and you'll make a difference.

I had a young woman call me on Mother's Day. Her mom—a negative-spirited woman—had bawled her out earlier that day because she didn't do what she wanted, hadn't taken care of something or other. So she yelled at her daughter. On Mother's Day.

My young friend called me up afterward in tears and said to me, "You're my spiritual mom. I wouldn't know Jesus if it wasn't for you. But . . . can you be my real mom today?"

It broke my heart. I said, "Yes, I'll be your real mom."

And she said, "Happy Mother's Day."

Those are the moments that make it all worth it. They're what matters. I tell all the women I work with that the goal is getting people to heaven. That's what we're doing here. Nothing supersedes it. Yes, we want everybody to grow up to be the best Christian wives, be the best Christian mothers, be the best witnesses to the Lord, and that's what I teach the ladies in my group. But if you have an opportunity and someone stands before you clearly in need, you never waste that opportunity to share God with her. You never choose otherwise. It's never not important. People need to know Jesus, and that's what we're going for. It's like a fire burning in me.

Two and half years ago, when we first found out we'd be doing the show [A&E *Duck Dynasty*], I was thrilled because I've always been proud of my family and was happy to share them with America. But I'll tell you, the very thought of not being able to work with my group, with my women . . . it just put me in tears. I prayed, *Please, God, don't take this away from me. Let me work it out.* And what's so amazing is that He did. He sent me faithful women I could depend on to step in and help so I wouldn't lose it all. I'm still able to mentor even though I'm busy with the show.

And so I do. I share God with whomever I can, whenever I can, as much as I can. My Nanny would be glad. I know I am. And I know God is too.

When I first began to work with Titus 2 mentoring, evangelism wasn't on my radar. I think you'd agree that when you hear the word *evangelism*, small group meetings might not come to mind. Someone preaching passionately at a tent meeting? Yes. A family doing mission work in a far-off country? Yes. A group handing out tracts on a street corner? Yes, these are time-tested methods of spreading the gospel.

On the other hand, when you think of small group mentoring, you think of many of the things we've covered in this book. How to be vulnerable. How to study God's Word. How to be empathetic. How to learn from each other . . .

But wait! *Learn from each other.* When you break it down to its simplest elements, that's what evangelism is, isn't it: showing others through word and deed who God is. So what we found—what Kay made abundantly clear to us—is that Titus 2 mentoring and evangelism go hand in hand. It's the type of evangelism found in our daily moments and interactions. The type of evangelism that effortlessly communicates God's love and engages others. And therefore the type of evangelism we hope to inspire in you, dear reader. Our goal is the portrayal of a deep and authentic relationship with God and the ability to share that relationship in whatever situation comes up, with whomever has a need. Showing Jesus to others doesn't have to be a formal event. As Kay's grandmother taught her, it should be as simple as living and breathing.

Here's an example. Each month our Titus 2 mentors give their young women a Bible verse that's studied during the meeting. One young woman always prints out the verse, along with a few words of encouragement, and takes it to work with her the next day. She makes copies and puts one on all her coworkers' desks. Nothing more than that—no conversations or explanation. Her coworkers come in that morning and find a short-and-sweet devotion on their desks.

Well, people love it. They've begun to anticipate it each week. And some of the ladies came forward and asked our young friend about where she's getting her verses and inspiration. She told them about her mentoring group, and they wanted in! Just like that she has taken what she learned in her group and modeled it to encourage others toward a relationship with God.

People crave those types of intentional interactions. Yet for whatever reason, many of them are not finding that interaction in traditional church settings. Actually, many feel they cannot come to church until they've first "fixed" their lives. So they're staying away from the very thing that could help them. That's one of the reasons that small groups—in a home setting—are working.

"So many people say, 'When I get my life right, I'm going to come back to church,'" agrees Kay. "Well, knowing God is how you get your life straight! And if you won't go to church to get to know Him—which many people won't—there has to be another way. That means we have to be the ones representing to these lost folks. Small groups work for that. They're less intimidating, more intimate than church. Small groups are an opportunity to break things down to the basics."

That's exactly it. Small groups are where relationships happen. They don't happen during a sermon at church. They happen during interactions over the week or month. And those moments are what keep us coming back to the church service on Sundays. It's like a bunch of little groups off the family tree meeting during the week and then joining up for the big family gathering at church. Because we've all been together during the week and seen each other and interacted in each other's lives, being together on Sunday is much more meaningful.

Again, this evangelism works simply through representing Christ to others in your group—or seeing them represent Him to you—and then taking that out your door to others. We can't be afraid to make that step. We can't worry about feeling inadequate or think we'll misrepresent God or His Word. We just have to get out there and love.

I cannot tell you the number of women who speak to me about how Kay has spent time with them, encouraging them. About the effort she puts into helping women get through whatever they're dealing with. As Kay told us, she did not have a great life for many years. She was not and is not a perfect woman. But she doesn't let that stop her. She takes her life experiences and wisdom and her passion for God and runs toward others instead of away. And women are finding hope because of that passion. They're finding God.

And Kay does make it effortless. She is an inspiration to many. I know this because I'm the one who places women in her mentoring group. Now, you have to understand: Kay and

Phil live pretty much out in the middle of nowhere, tucked into a bend in the river. It's at least a thirty-minute drive for many of her ladies and even more for some. So before I place anyone in her group I always call the woman to make sure she doesn't mind the drive. If someone prefers I can put her in someone else's group.

Not one woman I've ever called has said no to Kay's group. They all want to be in it, and they never want to leave it! That's the impact her no-holds-barred love has on people. She is a mom to so many women who would otherwise have none. She has spoken God's truth to so many who might otherwise have never heard.

That's the difference a Titus 2 ministry can make—the difference you can make in a person's life when you share who you are. When you share where you were and where you are now because of Him. Because as Kay says, it's never not important.

Heart Check

> I long to see you so that I may impart to you
> some spiritual gift to make you strong—that is,
> that you and I may be mutually encouraged by
> each other's faith.
>
> —Romans 1:11–12

Have you ever considered that small group mentoring could be a form of evangelism? What do you think about the possibilities that opens up?

_____

_____

_____

_____

Who is an older woman whose words and deeds spoke to you in meaningful ways in terms of your faith? What did she do to reach you?

_____

_____

_____

_____

Have you ever had an opportunity to evangelize and show God to someone else? Did you take that opportunity? Explain.

_____

_____

_____

_____

God, I realize evangelism comes in many shapes and situations. Help me find women who can teach and mentor me. Help me be aware of how I can show You to others. Because evangelism is never not important.

Our church has some unique dynamics. One is that our members live in about eight different towns and communities around the area, so we're really diverse and spread out. Another is that many people who attend our church are related. Therefore many families sit together at church and then leave together and eat together afterward. To me as a newcomer these issues created the feeling of "Sunday-only friends." I would not see a majority of my church family anywhere else except at a worship service. And even then many were busy with their own families.

My Titus 2 mentoring group really opened up the possibility for deeper relationships. Our church had women's ministries and Bible studies in the past but hadn't done anything in a couple of years due to lack of leadership and participation. Through the mentoring groups the women have really come together and become active in the church. Close relationships have formed.

In my first group I was with two young women I had only met at church. We came to know each other a lot better, especially because we were able to share some struggles going on in our lives. That made a big impact on our relationship, so much so that we got together even outside small group to have lunch, go to the pool—things we never would have done otherwise.

To me this is what our groups are all about: making connections and sharing our stories so that we can make a difference in each other's lives and become closer because of it. Small groups are important for churches. They create a feeling of community and family. We are supposed to be the body of Christ, and we must be united as one body. But the church cannot do that by just getting together once a week. Relationships must be formed and developed. Being in someone's home is a warm, welcoming environment that is better for connection, community, and spiritual growth than sitting in an auditorium.

I especially think small groups for women are important because women are social creatures and we need to get together to talk. I feel like a Titus 2 ministry is the perfect environment to do just that. The group members encourage each other and share wisdom from their personal experiences. They support and strengthen each other. For me, I know I grow more spiritually when I am sharing my faith and life experiences with others, when we are studying the Bible together and sharing our personal thoughts. It's a spiritual high for me.

In order to fight the sin and evil of this world, we have to stick together and be there for each other. In one of my small groups there was a young woman who was going through some hard things with her family. She was in a custody battle, her sister was living with her, and she was trying to work and go to school. She relied on our group for advice, comfort, prayers, and someone to listen to her.

I think in times like these, Christian women should meet and know each other well to support their peers. They have to be willing to share their own life experiences so they can minister to others.

—AMY, MENTEE

Being a part of a Titus 2 group is a life-changing experience. It creates a permanent bond among the women involved—both the mentors and the younger women—that comes only from having shared our life experiences with each other and ministered to each other through them. We make ourselves vulnerable to each other by exposing our true selves, sometimes in the hope we will be healed and sometimes in the hope we can heal others. Sharing like that doesn't just go away. It continues to grow. Anytime women connect with each other on a one-on-one basis, there is a strengthening of the group to which those individuals belong.

And that's a good thing because women need the friendship of other women. There is much to be gained in belonging to a compassionate, caring, and supportive group. It's a vital part of being able to share the love of Christ with each other. We all face many pressures in our lives, especially younger women. Body image issues, social issues, work or school or home issues—they all beat at us and weaken us. We need our small group relationships as a sort of shelter from the storm. I cannot tell you how many times I've seen women in the group reach out to others, wanting to help with their struggles. This is truly evangelism at its best—the simple sharing of God's love through relationships and the exposing of life experiences, good and bad.

I have had many opportunities to share my testimony through our Titus 2 ministry. At first it was not easy. My struggles were something I'd been taught to hide, something considered socially unacceptable to talk about. But I realized that every woman has her own issues. And if I as a mentor was unwilling to put my true self out there in hopes of helping others, how could I expect my girls to do the same? We have to lead by example. So I did. I have faith that God honored my commitment by blessing those young women's lives—and that they in turn have learned to have courage in sharing their own stories.

We will never know all the lives that have been touched and blessed by our Titus 2 ministry. But I know it is many. How could it not be, when we're so intentional in all we do? We create relationships that support and encourage each other. We give of ourselves in ways that forge emotional and spiritual bonds.

And even though we may not see each other often after the year has ended and the group has disbanded, we always have that special caring for each other. No matter where we see each other—in church or at other meeting places—we have an instant connection because of what we've given to each other, the joys and sorrows we've uncovered in our loving and caring group. That itself is worth the momentary struggles we face.

—CAROL, MENTOR

CHAPTER NINE

OPEN TO GROWTH

Be the Wife, Mom, and Woman You Deserve to Be

> Your problem is how you are going to spend this one and precious life you have been issued. Whether you're going to spend it trying to look good and creating the illusion that you have power over circumstances, or whether you are going to taste it, enjoy it and find out the truth about who you are.
>
> —*Anne Lamott*

MINDY'S STORY

I didn't grow up in the church. We were a holiday family—Easter, Christmas, the big ones. So although my parents raised us with good morals and values and my grandparents were active in their church, I never understood what a relationship with Jesus was about.

This served me just fine until the year I turned fifteen. That was the year my mother was murdered.

Yes, you read that right.

A week after my mother's death my father was arrested for that crime, and a year later he was convicted by a jury. Within a matter of a few months, my sister and I were orphaned. Our lives were turned upside down. My father was understandably focused on proving his innocence. And because everything revolved around that, my sister and I never really had the time to mourn my mother. She was there and then she was gone, and we were forced to move on and think about other things.

Perhaps for those reasons—and a longing for love that had no chance of being fulfilled on my current path—I married young, at eighteen. Had a child by the time I was nineteen. Was divorced by the time I was twenty. And then remarried and divorced again. I remember at the time I was desperate to feel connected to somebody, anybody. And I felt so confused about and ashamed of what my life had become. I was a young mother adrift in an unhappy life.

Thankfully, the train wreck of my marital life was halted when I met the man who would become my current husband. He was everything I hoped for and everything I needed. We just celebrated our twelfth anniversary this year.

Even more thankfully, it was during those years that I became involved with a Titus 2 ministry. Truthfully, I was pretty much told I needed to be a part of it. If anyone did, it was me! At the time I thought to myself, *Well, fine. Here we go again. Another women's group. What are we going to do this time?* But in hindsight I'm able to say it was much more than I ever dreamed it could be. The women in this ministry rescued me. They helped save my marriage. They helped rescue my children. And more than anything, they gave me the mother relationships I'd lost in my life. And ten years later I'm still involved in the ministry and still have those relationships.

Don't get me wrong—my paternal grandparents, with whom my sister and I lived at the time, were good people. We just didn't have a close relationship with them. And because of the situation with my mother's murder and father's conviction, we were limited in what we could share with my mother's parents. We had no perspective on which we could agree. So to fill the need, the various ladies in my mentoring groups throughout the years stepped in as surrogates.

I know without a shadow of a doubt that the Titus 2 model was created for me. I had so many needs back then it would have been impossible for just one mentor, one woman, to help me. But with so many to lean on and go to, it changed everything in the course of my life. Those incredible women taught me from the ground up how to be a wife and mother and friend, how to study the Bible and biblical truths, how to be open with others. I didn't really know how to have relationships with women, so I even learned that. Being in groups, being able to talk about things, being able to show my emotions . . . without my mentors I probably never would have done those. I was one of those tough gals who played sports. I was more comfortable with a slap on the back from the guys than a hug around the shoulder from the ladies.

Perhaps that, too, was a product of not growing up with a mom. I love my son dearly, but it wasn't until I had my own daughter that I truly began to understand what I'd lost—that special something a mother-daughter connection brings to your life. I had only flashes of memories left of my mom in my life—birthday parties and smells and such. And I could see in my interactions with my daughter that there was so much more than that.

But rather than allow me to wallow and mourn my loss, my mentors challenged me to step up and be the mom I'd never had, to move forward and build a close relationship with my daughter. They modeled what it looked like so that I could live it with her. They were like one-stop shopping for mommyhood. For example, they'd have something like a tea party theme for one of our small group meetings, with dresses and storybooks and all the food that went with it. "See?" they'd say. "You can do this with your daughter." And I'd say okay.

They'd teach us a cheer or how to draw with finger paint—all part of our small group lesson. "Now go home and do this with your kids," they'd encourage. Okay.

They showed me practical things like how to fix my daughter's hair and how to sew. (Well, actually, I went to one of them and begged her to show my daughter how to sew.)

Oh, the many things I've learned! I've been mentored by elders' wives and teachers and homemakers and more. Women with amazing abilities, women I stand in awe of. They taught us younger ones how to cook and organize a pantry, how to decorate a cake, how to follow a recipe or put on a dinner, how to be hospitable, how to study the Bible, how to nurture a husband, how to raise our kids. With their guidance, I've done things I never would have imagined doing. Crafts . . . which for an ex-sports player is taking it pretty far. I even learned how to arrange flowers!

With each mentor and each group of women I was a part of, I saw all the many attributes of what makes up the body of Christ. And what I needed to emulate to be the best woman and wife and mother I can be. Each mentor comes to a lesson in a different way, from a different perspective. But we all seek the same goal: to be a godly woman to the best of our ability. So they modeled what worked toward that goal in their own lives. We were all linking arms and taking the same path together.

None of this could have happened, of course, if I hadn't been open to my mentors' teachings, open to seeking out wise counsel and resources, unafraid to ask questions or express my needs. I might not always get the answer I wanted, and I might not be taught in the way I expected, but if they were willing to open themselves up and share from their experiences without shame, then I wasn't going to be ashamed of my needs, of divorce, of stepparenting issues, of what I felt were my failings. Besides, I had to remind myself to focus on what God wanted to teach me, not necessarily the reason I needed the help. Being reminded of that perspective was important.

And it's been such a blessing to be a part of these women's lives. When you go through things with each other, you create lifelong friendships. There are girls I didn't know a lot about until we were together in the group. And some of them are my closest friends now. I learned how to be a friend among these ladies. Learned how to trust and share and be vulnerable. Before our Titus 2 ministry I didn't even know what those things meant. Being emotionally and spiritually vulnerable is different from being a scared vulnerable, if that makes sense. It was hard for me. At first I felt like people saw me and thought, *Look at her—at how strong she is.* So I felt I had to be strong. But in reality, for years I'd been living a one-foot-in-front-of-the-other existence. I'd been in a fog. Staying plugged into these women was the only thing that kept me making those steps. And I got to the point where I could share that, expose that part of myself, admit I wasn't strong at all. It was a Spirit-led journey.

In the end, being part of a Titus 2 ministry hasn't been just one lesson, or even two or five. It's been many. It's been a continuous stream of challenges and modeling and encouragement and listening and teaching. And as I said, it's impacted every aspect of the woman I am today. This past year my son graduated from high school. He came to me asking whom he should send invitations to.

And I said, "We're going to send them to everybody who had a hand in where you are and where we are as a family." Three hundred-plus invitations later, we had to laugh. We realized he has way more "grandmothers" than I ever had. But we wouldn't change a thing. We licked every envelope with a smile.

One of the most precious pieces to me in all this has been seeing how my sister's life has been affected. She struggled terribly after we lost our parents. And I admit I pushed her a lot, trying so hard in my own way to knock some sense into her. It didn't work. But being a part of my mentoring group taught me a different way to handle that situation—how to approach her not from a surrogate mother point of view but as a sister. And not just a blood sister but a sister in Christ who wanted to mentor her as I'd been mentored. Instead of pushing her back into church, I loved her back in. And now she has a renewed life and an amazing husband.

I do have to laugh sometimes at all the things we've experienced and endured. And I'm thankful I'm able to. I'm grateful to have the context of understanding where I was, where I could've been, and where I am. I could be a mean and miserable woman, and it would be excusable. That's what people would say because of the things that happened in my life. "Oh, she can't help being bitter."

But my Titus 2 women say no. They challenge me. "You're not going to be the norm," they tell me. "You're going to be the exception." And then they set out to walk beside me every step of the way and make sure it happens. I will never be able to repay them for that. But the amazing thing is I don't need to. They do it for love of me and for love of a God who commands us to be the change we want to see. And in the years to come I will gladly, faithfully, joyfully return the favor.

It's the least I can do.

Mindy's story likely includes more trauma than you and I will ever know in our lives. Her story is definitely unique. But not in the way you'd expect. It's unique because in the face of almost insurmountable odds she found victory. There are many stories out there similar to hers, but they do not end well. Many, in fact, end very badly indeed. Mindy's doesn't—because of intentional intervention from and interaction with a group of loving women who were vested in her success. They took over what her mom and dad were not able to do anymore. These women all had a hand in every aspect of her life.

Thankfully, she was open to their help. Because when those women got ahold of her, they had a lot of work to do. Mindy was, shall we say, a bit rough around the edges. She didn't know anything about life or parenting. She had no clue how to stay in and grow a healthy marriage. She was a blank slate. But she had such a heart to learn. She was and is a fighter, and she refused to give up. She took being the best possible mom and wife and woman to heart, and she sought out those people who could meet her needs and make those things happen. And people respect her for that.

That's one reason I hold her up here—because she does have that attitude of wanting to be God's. She wants to know what it looks like to be a godly woman, what it looks like to be a mom raising a godly child, what it looks like to be a supportive wife. And I think that attitude of being teachable has been key to her success. Mindy's an athlete, and I'm sure her coaches would say she's coachable. Through Titus 2 mentoring she has been coached in life skills—in eternal skills.

And it's not like she's one of those people who just follows the crowd with no thought for what she's doing. She is a strong-willed woman, and her choices are intentional.

Mindy agrees. "I committed myself to being open. To saying, 'I don't know. Please help me. Please tell me what to do and how to do it.' My husband, Michael, and I never sat back and said, 'Let's see what happens.' We worked at it. And we were specific, too, in our end goal. The thing that kept us going was our children and our desire to create a better family future for them. Both Michael and I have been divorced. His parents were divorced. My parents struggled. So we were determined we were going to make it and provide a successful and godly model for our kids growing up. That was great motivation for me."

Mindy's determination was the first half of her success. The other was the people who were willing to support her and give her answers and help and advice and walk beside her through a tough time in her life. She had a major resource right at her fingertips—phone numbers and relationships. And that was not by accident. I wrote the plans for the Titus 2 ministry, Heart to Home, with Mindy in mind, because I looked at her and knew she needed help—more help than any one woman could give her. We had to do something different, give her something and someone at every stage of her fight.

So that's what we did. Using the words and teachings of Titus 2, we created a ministry centered around two things: the willingness of older women to be involved in relationships and the willingness of young women to be encouraged and supported and loved and taught and trained and guided. Doing this brought a whole new dimension to mentoring, something shared among many people, each adding to the flavor and dynamic and synergy of the conversation, each pushing toward a common goal.

It took that combination to work in Mindy's life. And if we could meet Mindy's needs, we could meet anyone's.

Mindy has come so far from where she was, has climbed so far out of that hole she was stuck in. I know Satan was sitting there rubbing his hands and thinking, *I've got this girl.* I know he was thinking there was no way Mindy could overcome the trauma she'd endured and the multiple bad decisions that had dragged her down. Satan thought he'd severed her ties with God.

But Mindy just laughed at him. "No," she said. "You don't have me, and you don't have my family." And she dug in her heels and clung to the helping hands of the mentors who gathered around her.

God clung to her and made sure she had what she needed. It reminds me of one of my favorite parables, when the shepherd left the ninety-nine sheep and went out to find the one who was lost. He had one of his charges out there, and he was going to rescue that sheep no matter what. Matthew 18:13–14 says, "And if he finds it, truly I tell you, he is happier about that one sheep than about the ninety-nine that did not wander off. In the same way your Father in heaven is not willing that any of these little ones should perish."

I really believe that's what happened to Mindy. She was God's child, and He went after her and pulled her back in. And now we all see the legacy of faith renewed with her and her husband. Such a remarkable testament to the faithfulness of God—and to the many women who made sure Mindy stayed in His strength.

This is where we come full circle. We began our journey with Maranda's story, seeing a young woman taking her first steps in vulnerability, choosing to open herself up to a group of loving women and be changed by them. We end part 1 of this book here, with Mindy's story, seeing in her the fulfillment of all a Titus 2 ministry can bring to a woman's—to your—life.

If nothing else, dear reader, I hope you take away with you this truth: God reaches us through each other. The Word of God is here and the Holy Spirit is here, but God's plan is that we embody His lessons and teachings. We are to take care of each other. We are to love each other. We are to support each other, train each other, guide each other, teach each other.

God entrusts us with modeling to each other what faith looks like. And that means more than just being a good example to others once a week in church. To truly impact another's life, we have to be together often enough and intimately enough to make a difference. Research shows that the strongest, most vibrant churches are those with thriving small group ministries. What better way to begin than with a Titus 2 ministry, with the privilege of impacting not just one life but many.

So that's my challenge to you, my friend: take that step and either find a Titus 2 mentoring ministry near you or create one. I believe you've seen from the stories we've shared the impact it can have on your lives. Are you up for it? Because I promise you won't be disappointed.

In the next section of the book we will look at how to go about building a Titus 2 ministry from the ground up. Be forewarned—by its very nature it is not a solitary task. So be prepared to reach out to your friends, your church ladies, and others. Once you begin to convey what's waiting for them, I think it will be an easy undertaking.

I'm excited for you—excited for all the possibilities, for all I know you will experience. Get ready to be transformed!

Heart Check

He commanded our ancestors
  to teach their children,
so the next generation would know [His statutes],
  even the children yet to be born,
  and they in turn would tell their children.

—Psalm 78:5-6

So you're ready for a Titus 2 ministry. What's the first step you will take toward mentoring when you put down this book? How does that make you feel?

_____

_____

_____

_____

In moving forward with this opportunity, what changes do you hope to see in your life?

_____

_____

_____

_____

What do you think your favorite part of a Titus 2 ministry will be? Explain.

_____

_____

_____

_____

Lord, You've made it clear that You inhabit godly group mentoring—that You desire for us to have relationships in these settings. Guide me as I seek to find a place among Your women. I am ready to be the wife, mom, friend, and woman You want me to be. I am ready to be transformed.

Our church has always had a loving congregation and a bustling and busy ministry. But in spite of our activities, the women of the congregation were missing an overall connection. We couldn't quite put a finger on it, but we felt—we knew—something was missing: It was frustrating. We all had our own individual desires for what a ministry should look like, and none of them was being fulfilled. I know the younger women in the church were especially affected by this.

Finally, we realized that although we had Bible study groups, they were all age- and life-stage related. The different groups were isolated, which caused gaps in our unity and a stumbling block to our relationships. We needed something different.

So we chose to begin a Titus 2 ministry, linking women across age barriers in a conscious effort to make connections and mentor each other. I'm happy to say that ministry has transformed our church and created a platform that allows us to grow in our roles as women of God. It has gently redirected us and focused us on His desires for us. It's been a real eye-opening experience—not only for me but for all the women. Especially the young ladies.

Personally, I love what my own role has been in the process. To me, Titus 2 is a challenge, an expectation from God that has been presented to the older women. It's a spiritual reality check, directing us to strive for deeper relationships with each other. I think we've all realized the importance and responsibility of our place in God's plan. We have a significant role: to help leave a legacy through sharing our experiences while encouraging the younger women to seek God's wisdom at each step in life. Not only that, but we are charged with being mindful of our own spiritual health so that we can be effective teachers of what is good to those in different stages of life. That's something I never put much thought into—that I need to be spiritually fit before I can coach someone else. It really puts things into perspective. But I think we've all risen to the challenge.

And we've all seen and felt a different vibe in our church community as we've implemented the program. I love how the older women have taken the initiative, reaching out to the younger women through a desire to share their hearts, values, and lives. And the younger women have responded as they've felt the care and support and attention given to them. They are opening up their lives to each other, growing closer. They are being uplifted and spiritually encouraged. They are being challenged, growing in understanding of God's plan for them as women and their roles in His kingdom. And they are learning so much—both the important spiritual lessons and the practical skills they will need moving forward in their lives.

Women of all ages in our church are excited to be a part of our Titus 2 small groups. That energy, and the results we're seeing, show we are moving in the right direction. I can't wait to see over time just how much this mentoring ministry will bless and enrich not only the women involved but our congregation as a whole.

—KIM, MENTOR

As a mom of two young daughters, my Titus 2 group has been a blessing in my life. The opportunity to be served a home-cooked meal on a monthly basis is enough to draw any frazzled mom, but that's not why I attend. I attend because I enjoy the fellowship and the investment the mentors are making in my life as a Christian woman, as a wife, and as a mother.

I believe this ministry was very much needed in our church. There was a growing disconnect between the older generation and the younger. Neither side knew how to remedy the problem until Titus 2 made its way into our lives. I am so thankful it did! Beforehand, I knew only a handful of the older women, but now I feel a connection to them and am delighted when I see them in worship services, community projects, or just around town.

I also feel connected with my peers. Each season that I've been in our Titus 2 groups, I have been put into a new small group where I did not know most of the women. Rather than feeling uncomfortable, it has been refreshing to meet these women and develop relationships I probably would not have had outside of our Titus 2 ministry. It shows me how God's plan is at work to bring new and meaningful friendships into my life.

And it continues outside the one night a month that we get together. Between meetings the women in our Titus 2 group share prayer requests and pray for each other throughout the month, whether it's for health or medical issues, work-related matters, or struggles we have as moms. We keep in touch through Facebook to keep abreast of certain outcomes or praises. We make plans to visit with each other or go out for meals. We look for each other at church. This ministry has really enriched our lives in terms of new friendships and support.

And speaking of support, the mentors dote on us for the entire night. Yes, the time we spend with God and the Word and fellowship is important. But oh, the joy of being pampered for a night! No cooking, no food to cut up for my children, no dishes to clean or tables to sweep under. Add to that the adult conversations with no interruptions. I love sharing time with my family, but it's a nice break to be the center of attention once a month at our meetings. The mentors start off each meeting with fellowship and a fun craft or game, then a delicious meal, followed by dessert and a time of devotion. At the end of the meeting we're given a "happy" to take home with us, and if for some reason we miss the meeting, they'll even deliver our "happy" to us!

No doubt about it: I've been blessed by our mentors' generosity and genuine love for us. And I've seen the difference that the support and teaching and loving they give us—and that they foster in each of us for each other—has made in our lives. It's been an incredible journey.

—APRIL, MENTEE

PART TWO

Making It Happen

God did not create you to be alone. He deposited skills, knowledge, and talents in someone out there who is expected to mentor you, teach you and encourage you to go high. Go, get a mentor!
—*Israelmore Ayivor*

CHAPTER TEN

NEXT STEPS

What Do I Do Now?

> Studies show that generally speaking, the
> strongest drive for females is connection.
> Our needs for attachment are strong,
> and we need God's wisdom and power
> to overcome unhealthy patterns. But in
> Christ we can overcome the pain, break the
> chains, and unleash a gift that will bless not
> only us, but also generations to come.
> —*Dee Brestin*

Are you inspired yet? Do you want to rush right out and start your own Titus 2 mentoring group? Are you itching to find others to join with you? I certainly hope so. It's impossible to read the stories of how intentional mentoring relationships transformed these lovely women's lives and not want to experience the same thing. Or at least something similar. And you're not alone in feeling this way. Remember, many of the women in the stories—and hundreds of other women with whom I've connected—at some point felt the same way you do. And they did something about it.

That's where you are right now. Craving something different. Ready for a change. Looking for relationships with like-minded women. Wanting more.

So let's look at what you can do to make it happen. For our purposes, we're going to assume your plan is to create a Titus 2 ministry from scratch. I encourage you, though, to check around your community or city and see if something like this is already up and running. You may find just what you're looking for already alive and thriving and all you need to do is plug in.

But in case that opportunity is not available, here are the next steps you can take. Note that part 2 of this book is an interactive guide. I encourage you to jot things down as you work your way through each section. Doing so will not only provide instant feedback and direction but will be a resource you can return to down the road, to remind you of what you envisioned and how you hoped to accomplish it.

Pray

First, pray. Pray a lot. Pray for guidance, for understanding and insight, for God's blessing on your endeavor. Pray to Him about your desires and hopes and dreams and needs. Ask Him to send just the right women to join with you—the ladies who will enrich your life, the ladies He knows you'll enrich.

Then pray some more. You know as well as I that no matter what we do to create a mentoring relationship, God needs to be there first. Allow Him to guide you in your steps. As James said, "If any of you lacks wisdom, you should ask God, who gives generously to all without finding fault, and it will be given to you" (1:5). God's got your back. So be intentional in what you're asking for.

Write your prayer requests here:

_____

_____

_____

_____

_____

Study

Next, get out your Bible and read what God has to say to you about women and relational ministries. You're getting ready to place your spiritual life into another woman's hands. Have you considered what that means? You don't want to go willy-nilly and set up this relationship without thinking it through. When you need a financial adviser, you don't just pick the first one listed in the phone book or Google and do whatever they tell you, right? When you're learning how to rock climb, you don't find a guy sitting on top of a cliff and ask him to hold your rope while you try it out, do you? I didn't think so.

Thankfully, we have a lot of wisdom packed into a single guide—the Bible. And some very specific words about how God wants us to lean on each other as His people. In the introduction we walked through the verses in Titus 2. Flip to it one more time and let's read it together:

Likewise, teach the older women to be reverent in the
way they live, not to be slanderers or addicted to much
wine, but to teach what is good. Then they can urge the
younger women to love their husbands and children, to
be self-controlled and pure, to be busy at home, to be
kind, and to be subject to their husbands, so that no
one will malign the word of God. (vv. 3–5)

So what does this passage mean? In a nutshell, this is an easy
explanation of what God hopes for in a mentoring relationship.
In Titus 2, the apostle Paul is first asking older women to be
focused on God. And then he's saying that when they are—when
women understand that all wisdom ultimately comes from
Him—then they are to impart that wisdom to the younger generation. Mentoring is a mandate! And not just for the mentors.
You as the mentee are tasked with learning from them. Not simply so that you will have knowledge of all the many ways—spiritual, practical, or otherwise—to foster a healthy marriage and
home life, but so that you will be a solid and accurate representation of God's Word. You are His living representatives of faith.

Do the words of Titus 2 put things in a different perspective for
you? Explain.

_____

_____

_____

_____

Grab a Friend

So now that you've realized how important this whole mentoring relationship will be, you need to begin to find like-minded women to join you in this adventure. Take a moment to list some friends and acquaintances you feel fit the bill. I encourage you to make this a short list for now. You want to make sure you are 100 percent on the same page with what this mentoring ministry will look like, and a multitude of different opinions may end up overwhelming you right off the bat.

Once you have your list, choose the one woman on it whom you believe will immediately and absolutely jump onboard, and approach her.

Write your list of like-minded women here:

_____

_____

_____

_____

Now choose the one you feel should take the first step with you. Why are you choosing her?

_____

_____

_____

_____

Brainstorm

The next step is to arrange to meet with the woman you chose and share with her your mission, your goals, your dreams for a Titus 2 group. Ask her about hers. Talk it through. Brainstorm ideas, write them down, then study them. Are they accurate? Doable? Write up a short-term plan for making them happen.

And—you guessed it—pray! Pray for God's hand in every aspect of what you're attempting. Cover yourself in the Holy Spirit's protection and blessing.

What are your goals and dreams for a Titus 2 group?

_____

_____

_____

_____

_____

_____

What's your game plan for implementing them?

_____

_____

_____

_____

_____

_____

Grab More Friends

Now you have a Titus 2 partner. Head back to your list and pick a few more women (including any your partner may have to add) and do the whole thing over again. Consolidate your desires for what you want as a group.

Remember: Within this ministry you will not only be learning from your mentor and studying God's Word. You will be baring your hearts and souls, perhaps revealing things you've never shared with anyone. You'll be making yourselves vulnerable before others. So you need to feel confident about and secure with this initial group of ladies you're gathering. Down the road, as the ministry grows, you will likely have many women joining whom you don't know, and you'll all be committing to vulnerability together. But for now, consider sticking with a select group you're comfortable with.

Have any of your original goals and desires for the Titus 2 group changed? Explain.

_____

_____

_____

_____

Find a Titus 2 Mentor

Remember, until this point we've been talking about mentees—those women who, like you, crave the wisdom and guiding hand

HEARTFELT

of a mentor. Now it's time to seek out at least one potential mentor. Again, this is someone your group will intentionally consider and choose, someone you all feel confident in and want to be a part of what you're doing. You should all feel comfortable with her. It's understandable that not everybody in your group may know her at this point, but those who don't should feel confident in the guidance and advocacy of their peers.

Approach your potential mentor and talk with her. Explain your desires for a Titus 2 relationship with her. Show her your plans. More important, show her the words from Titus 2 and talk them through with her. Is she like-minded about them? Does she understand the significance and weight of what her role would be? What are her own hopes and desires for younger women? Do they mesh with your own? How does she feel about things you all expect to learn from her? Is she willing to enter into this ministry with you?

This is a crucial step for all of you. The mentor you choose—and her commitment to the relationship—will color your future endeavors. You need to be sure everyone is onboard.

And don't forget: pray, pray, pray with her and the other women.

Write down your list of potential Titus 2 mentors here:

_____

_____

_____

_____

Now choose one of them to approach. How easy or hard was it to decide as a group on which name to put here? Explain.

_____

_____

_____

_____

Plan

Hopefully at this point your prospective mentor has agreed to join you on this journey. Now come the practical aspects of creating a Titus 2 ministry. Here are some things to consider:

- Where do you all envision this mentoring group meeting? I encourage you to base it out of a home—not because we don't want churches involved but because we want to make sure everyone feels at ease. And if we're honest, we'll admit sometimes women feel intimidated or inhibited by meetings held at a church building.

- How will your church(es) support you? Just because the meetings aren't held in a church building doesn't mean the church can't offer support. What do you envision a church's support looking like? What do you need from them?

- What are the nuts and bolts of the program you want to create? This is an important one. How often will you meet (I suggest once a month during your usual school year) and for how long each time? Will you include meals (I recommend so)? What materials will you use—a pre-packaged Bible study or something your mentor creates? What teaching and study methods will be incorporated? Do you need more than one mentor for the group?

- How will you approach more mentees? How many do you want? Will you need more than one mentor group? (If so, you'll need to repeat all the above steps.) Will you have a formal registration process?

Of course there are other steps you may include. But the basics should be pretty straightforward. Be aware, though, that you will not think of everything. No one can. Flexibility will be key as you come upon unexpected questions or bumps in the road. The main thing is to approach with love, patience, and excitement the various aspects of the setup and work together to accomplish them.

And say it with me: pray!

What is your short list of necessary steps for implementing your Titus 2 group? Who will handle each?

_____

_____

_____

_____

_____

_____

Do you see any potential pitfalls or obstacles? Explain. How will you overcome them?

_____

_____

_____

_____

_____

_____

Release Control

Ah, now comes the part where you step back and assume the roles of mentees. You've chosen your mentor. You've worked together to create a model of what you envision your group to be. You've laid the groundwork for its spiritual and practical focus. Now you need to be confident enough in your planning to release yourselves into your mentor's hands and accept her leadership. Be empowered by this! Embrace where it leads you!

How does this step make you feel? Explain.

_____

_____

_____

_____

_____

_____

Make It Happen

In the end, it all comes down to the moment of truth. You've envisioned this thing called a Titus 2 ministry. You've planned for it. You've prayed about it and taken it to God for His hand in it. You're ready. Now breathe life into it. Enter with these women into the relationship with ready hearts, solid expectations, and the knowledge that you're fulfilling God's desires for all of you. Each of your journeys will be different. Each group will be different, as the various personalities of mentors and mentees intermingle. But you'll move forward secure in the knowledge that you're right where you need to be, learning and growing and experiencing something life changing. We've used the word *transform* a lot. Do prepare to be transformed. You will be.

In the next chapter I'm going to introduce you to a Titus 2 model that has already been set up, used, and proven. I am not saying you need to follow this exact model, only that you may find it practical and applicable to your group. You are welcome to adapt it in whatever way to suit your particular needs.

Heart Check

The things you have heard me say in the presence of many witnesses entrust to reliable people who will also be qualified to teach others.
                                    —2 Timothy 2:2

After reading this chapter, what do you see as the most
exciting step in creating a Titus 2 ministry? Explain.

_____

_____

_____

_____

Now consider what you feel will be the most difficult
step. Why is that? What are your plans for overcoming
this obstacle?

_____

_____

_____

_____

_____

Did you already have women in mind to begin this journey with you? Was it easy to think of who you wanted by your side? Difficult? Explain.

_____

_____

_____

_____

_____

Father, I am excited for what my future holds in terms of a mentoring community of women. I know You have plans for me and for the other women involved. Guide us as we seek to embody the words of Titus 2. My desire is that we honor You in all we do.

CHAPTER ELEVEN

THE TITUS 2 MODEL
Heart to Home

A mother is the truest friend we have, when trials
heavy and sudden, fall upon us; when adversity
takes the place of prosperity; when friends who
rejoice with us in our sunshine desert us; when
trouble thickens around us, still will she cling
to us, and endeavor by her kind precepts and
counsels to dissipate the clouds of darkness, and
cause peace to return to our hearts.
—*Washington Irving*

Congratulations, dear reader! You've made it through the book. You've hopefully gained a lot of helpful insights into just how much a Titus 2 small group can offer you on many levels. You've seen the steps you'll need to take to get yourself ready for a small group. Now, as I said, we'll take a look at all the details of an active small group, including the different parts of the meeting.

I want to offer a suggestion: Until this point everything in this book has been geared specifically toward you as a mentee. This chapter, which deals with the logistics of meetings, is where things become a guide for your mentor. So if you have one woman (or more) who has already agreed to shepherd you in this adventure, you might want to hand the book over to her now, because this is all information she's going to want to have. If you're not yet to the point of having a mentor, don't worry—this chapter can still be helpful for you. If nothing else, it will give you insight into just how hard your mentors will be working on your behalf.

Now then, let's take a look.

Introduction to Heart to Home

Throughout this book you've seen everyone refer to their small groups as Titus 2 ministries. And that's what they are. However, they are all based on the original program I put together, which is called Heart to Home. The women in my community have been using and sharing this program for more than ten years. Not only that, but the model has spread across the country; I travel all over the United States leading workshops on how to set up Heart to Home ministries in communities big and small. So for this chapter I'll be using that name—Heart to Home—as we discuss how to set up a small group and a meeting.

Too, you've seen all the women in this book referred to as *mentors* and *mentees*. Within the Heart to Home family, these ladies are called *Heart Moms* and *Heart Sisters*. I very intentionally chose those titles because more than anything I wanted to convey what the relationships are between these women—mother to daughter for the intergenerational mentoring relationships and sister to sister for the younger peers. I cannot stress enough how meaningful these titles are to everyone involved. The younger ladies truly consider their Heart Moms to be their spiritual moms. And the younger ones love and support their Heart Sisters like the best of family.

Both of these titles also relate to another key aspect of Heart to Home: the idea of meeting in the Heart Moms' homes rather than churches. Again, we're talking about a highly relational ministry. So the names are a perfect fit. We'll be using them as we talk through the elements of the program.

Heart Groups

What is a Heart Group? These small groups meet in homes once a month, hosted by Heart Moms. Everyone is there for a meal, a Bible study, prayer, and fellowship. The Heart Moms teach and inform the younger women through lessons and through examples. They are also personally modeling the behaviors.

Hospitality is a key lesson, demonstrated through meal preparation and the sharing of the home. Later on in the evening, biblical lessons include topics such as Christian living, parenting, and marriage. The loving and supportive relationships that are built within these Heart Groups will support the Heart Sisters long after the season is over.

Heart Moms

Heart Moms are godly women who have agreed to guide and influence a group of younger ladies. The age—well, we like to say that they are mature, not old. How old? Well, if you are a woman whose children have graduated from high school, or the age where that would be possible if you had kids, then you are old enough—or, as we prefer to say, mature enough—to be a Heart Mom. So, as a mature and caring woman with faith in your heart, you can bless a younger woman as a Heart Mom.

Heart Moms can share their home and model hospitality. They teach by example what a Christian household can look like. Despite all the differences that various personalities make in individual households, there are some consistent biblical guides that shape all Christian women's families and home lives. Heart Moms disciple their young charges through specific lessons concerning our roles as women—particularly as wives and mothers.

I'd like to note that our Heart Groups (and all Titus 2 ministries) have many single women involved as well. We do not forget them. Single women are storing up all the lessons they learn for the day when they may be married and have children of their own. And if they never marry or have children, they will still be in a family or with friends who will. All of us as God's women need to know and understand God's teachings regarding marriage and family and the Christian walk. We never know where or when that information will be a blessing or support for a loved one.

Heart Moms have stored up a wealth of wisdom during their personal faith journeys. They share the joys and disappointments, troubles and successes, tips and pitfalls they've learned. Their goal is to pass along the legacy of a Christian life through instruction and example.

Heart Moms have different roles. They can be a Host Mom who prepares a meal in her home, a Helper Mom in another woman's home, or a Bible Teacher Heart Mom who teaches the lesson.

Heart Sisters

Heart Sisters are the younger women whose lives are transformed by a Heart to Home Titus 2 ministry. They are Christian wives and/or mothers, single moms, or single young women. This is, therefore, more of a stage than an age. Sisters are still at the stage of life where they are, or could be, bearing, caring for, and raising children. These young women as Heart Sisters agree to commit to a Heart Group for a season of Heart to Home. They know they are there to learn about and grow in their faith, and that they're building a support system for each other. They will get as much out of it as they put into it.

Heart Sisters are the guests of honor at a Heart Mom's home, there to enjoy the hospitality, good food, friendship, fellowship, and Bible study offered to them.

Something helpful to Heart Moms is a Heart Sister information sheet that can be completed during the first meeting and kept by the Heart Moms for the remainder of the season. This can list basic information that includes contact information as well as extras such as birthdays and anniversaries, favorites (color, restaurant, perfect vacation, etc.), and a few key questions regarding what the Sisters hope to get out of the meetings.

Preparing for a Heart Group Meeting

Now let's take a look at some of the prep work done to facilitate a Heart Group meeting. Keep in mind these are informational but also flexible. They are suggestions that can be adapted for each program's needs.

Registration

If you are planning a Titus 2 mentoring program, it may be useful to know that the Heart to Home season typically runs during a school year (usually from September to May, excluding December, which is filled with holiday tasks and trips). A school-year calendar seems to be very helpful to the many moms involved. There could be a registration period the month before you begin meeting in your groups. It is helpful to hold the registration somewhere in your church building on several different days. A registration form that gives all the necessary information for planning and contact purposes is very useful.

I suggest including a clause in the registration form that explicitly asks Heart Sisters to commit their time to the group for the entire season. This is important, as a Sister who shows up only occasionally or intermittently will soon fall behind the rest of the Sisters in the relational aspects of the group. Too, one of the goals of Heart to Home is teaching the Sisters about honoring commitments. That said, it's understood there will always be several Heart Sisters who may not stay through a whole season for a variety of reasons. But for the ones who stay, committing to attending the once-a-month meetings is essential.

Still, I encourage you to be very careful and considerate in understanding that young mothers especially may struggle with regular attendance. Nursing infants, sick toddlers, and unreliable child care can create real challenges for these women, and we need to be sympathetic to their situations. I remember those days well, as you may.

Group Distribution

Once the registration period is over, the Heart Mom(s) should carefully consider all the women on the list. A Heart Group typically has eight to ten Sisters in it. Depending on the number of women signed up, more groups may be needed. Each Heart Group will also have three to four Heart Moms who are in charge of leading. Along with the Heart Sisters assigned, this will make the groups anywhere from twelve to fourteen in total number. Experience has shown me it is a rare night when every group member is able to be present. It sure is nice when it happens, though!

If there are to be multiple groups, consideration can be given to the different personalities involved, where the young women are in their lives, and the types of needs they may have. This is where a previous relationship with at least some of the Heart Moms will come in handy, since they may be aware of specific issues in a Heart Sister.

Small Group Rules

The Heart to Home program has very few rules. The goal is to foster spontaneous interaction between Moms and Sisters, so we do not want to put limits or restrictions on any part of the mentoring groups. But it's important to set a few basic house rules that facilitate the best in small group meetings. These rules are non-negotiable and are important for the good health of the group.

- *No children.* Heart Group meetings are for women only. Heart Sisters need this time to relax without the responsibilities of the home. They're there to be renewed and refreshed in mind and spirit. Moms can be a blessing if they will help any Sisters who are looking to find baby-sitters. Suggestions of older teens, adult women, or other moms who could help out with child care during the meetings would be very appreciated.

- *No gossip.* A crucial aspect of meetings is the knowledge that everything revealed during the meeting is off-limits to the rest of the world. This is a sacred and intimate time of sharing, and all the women involved need to have no fear of repercussions, regardless of what they may say. I've found that having a confidentiality agreement signed by all group members is useful. This can be comforting to the Sisters, as it's a reminder they are safe to share personal stories within their Heart Group, knowing these will not be shared outside of the group.

- *Share time.* For true, authentic communication to be the standard, for intimate and close relationships to build, the Heart Sisters need to feel they have equal time for sharing. So it's important for the Moms to monitor discussions and keep conversations flowing between all the women, not just the ones who enjoy talking or want to share a lot.

- *No counseling.* Although Heart Groups foster close relationships and allow Moms and Sisters to share very personal issues or needs, the meetings should not become counseling sessions. Focus is on encouragement, study, prayer, and fellowship and not on personally advising or counseling one woman. Any Sister who is especially struggling with a problem or crisis can be followed up on by a Heart Mom after the meeting.

Heart Moms will find the above rules helpful in maintaining a balance during meetings. Of course sensitivity to an individual Sister's needs is important, and the Moms may find they need to talk with her outside the meeting to offer comfort and prayer or to refer her to outside help. I've found it's very helpful to have readily available the names and contact information for several Christian counselors or wise advisers like pastors or family-life ministers.

Heart Group Meeting Schedule

A meeting usually lasts between two and a half to three hours, although the flow of the evening will sometimes dictate otherwise. Something to keep in mind is not having the meeting too soon (give them time to take care of dinner for the family) or too late (they're busy and weary women!). A good time for starting meetings is typically 6:30 or 7:00 p.m.

Within the meeting are several key elements. A typical meeting involves the following:

- Welcome and "get to know you" activity (15 minutes)
- Cooking demonstration or recipe sharing (45 minutes)
- Meal and dinner table talk (45 minutes)
- Bible study and Heart Mom moment (45 minutes)
- Take-home gift or favor and good-byes (5 minutes)

There are also special activities Heart Moms may schedule for particular meetings, depending on the season. Things like games, ice breakers, and other "get to know you" activities are useful especially during the first few meetings as the women are being introduced to one another. It is also a fun idea to plan for this kind of entertainment during holidays or special times.

Heart Group Meeting Preparations

A lot of preparation goes into each meeting. Things the Heart Moms need to be mindful of include:

- A date and time for the meeting
- A schedule for the evening
- A menu plan
- Food preparation (including assigning parts to other Heart Moms)
- Teacher plan for the lesson
- Theme and table decorations
- Gifts or favors for Heart Sisters to take home
- Invitations

These and other items will need to be prepared carefully by Heart Moms so that the meeting can occur without mishap or interruption. Again, the goal is to provide a stress-free night for the Sisters, so the better prepared the Moms are, the better for everyone involved. You want to present and model a gracious host. (Although if a mishap does occur, it provides a great teaching moment for that "Oh well, burned the beans" lesson! And believe me, it will happen.)

Meals and Menu Planning

Heart Moms should keep in mind that planning meals in advance helps all the leaders feel more comfortable. It also helps in distributing the responsibilities of all the preparations as well as planning for the costs of the meals, etc. Some tips:

- Pick a theme (e.g., Western, Make-Your-Own Pizza, Pasta Night, Salad Supper). This makes it fun to plan as well as helps organize and manage the events of the evening when you can coordinate everything. Watch your expenses, however.
- Make shopping lists for the menu in order to delegate food assignments.
- Family fare is preferred over fancy meals. The idea is to share your home, not feel like a restaurant.
- Buffet serving is fine, but make sure to seat all the women around a table if at all possible. The goal is to foster togetherness and sharing.

There are many, many websites and books out there on the topic of themed evenings. Heart Moms will want to do what they can to make the night memorable for their Heart Sisters.

Leading a Heart Group Meeting

Now we're down to the nitty-gritty—the actual Heart Group meeting. Following are the various elements that make up the whole. Again, while Heart to Home follows this specific plan, please know you are free to adapt the various parts to your needs.

"Get to Know You" Activity

Heart Group meetings often include fun games or activities. Every Sister, no matter her age, enjoys taking time to be a little silly . . . while still learning useful tips. For example, a lesson planned around a children's book or craft will give the Heart Sister something she can do with her own children. One of the first activities the Sisters will encounter is the "get to know you" game during each of the first few meetings. This is designed to break the ice among a group of women who may not know each other. A few examples include:

- Sharing how they met their husband/fiancé/boyfriend. (If your group includes single women, consider an alternate question that doesn't put them on the spot.)
- Having each Sister write down answers to key questions about herself (job, hobby, hometown, favorite movie/book/vacation), then redistributing them without revealing who they are and having Sisters guess who they describe.
- The tried-and-true question: "If you could have dinner with anyone, past or present, who would it be?"

Heart Moms can have fun with these activities. There are many icebreaker books and ideas online to choose from. Whatever you choose to use, it should serve the purpose of beginning to unite Heart Sisters through revealing each other's stories.

Cooking Demo, Recipe, and Meal

One of the main goals of Heart to Home is to teach practical life skills to the younger generation. Especially in these days of busyness and disjointed families, young women are not learning the skills they need to successfully care for a home and family. It is the reality of life in the twenty-first century, but it's nevertheless a sad fact. God desires that we as women be good stewards of our households and caretakers to our loved ones. As mentors, we want to model that it is a privilege to minister to our husbands and children through our homes.

Meals are an important part of that! Therefore, Heart Group meetings are set around dinner. During this time, Heart Moms demonstrate cooking and kitchen skills as well as other hospitality-related proficiencies, such as how to set a table, plan a menu, and stock a pantry.

Heart Moms also highlight the recipes used for the evening. Many Moms choose to print out the recipes on cards for the Sisters to take home and begin a collection.

The meal itself is a time of fellowship. Moms take special care to pamper the Sisters, serving the meal and cleaning up afterward. From the moment they walk in the door, no Sister should have to lift a finger to do anything related to the meal preparation and cleaning up! This element of the Heart Group evening is very valued by the Heart Sisters, who at this busy stage of life are accustomed to bringing a dish, serving on a cleanup committee, or being responsible for the event. They do not have to do any of that in Heart to Home. We want them to feel loved, nurtured, and cared for—just like a mom welcoming her grown daughter back home for a visit. These young women are special to us, and we want every part of the evening to show them we feel that way.

Dinner Table Talk

During the meal, Heart Moms direct the conversation by using questions designed to get everyone to know each other better. Heart Sisters may not be used to taking time for conversation during a meal—many homes today don't even have regular family meals. So the dinner table talk time is geared toward fostering a relational atmosphere. Conversation serves the group best when it is encouraging, helpful, and *fun*!

To ensure that all ladies have a moment to talk, Heart Moms can facilitate conversation with planned questions or conversation starters. All Sisters could answer the same question or each could answer her own individual question. It's also fun to hear from the Heart Moms as they are being introduced to the younger women.

Here are some suggestions for questions that could be used:

- Share about someone who has mentored you and how she did it.
- What is your favorite holiday and why?
- What is a big blessing in your life right now?
- What is your favorite thing about having children (or what is the thing you're most looking forward to when you do have children)?

Again, you will find many good ideas for icebreaker conversations online and in group activities books. Or use your own creativity to come up with ways to get the Sisters sharing at the table time.

It's important to say again that dinner table talk is a time specifically geared to allow *every* Sister to talk. Some judicious monitoring may need to be done to make sure a Sister doesn't overdo the talking or a shy Sister doesn't try to skip her turn. Help one who just can't find a way to end her answer by kindly recognizing her contribution, then chiming in if she goes too long to say, "Thanks so much for sharing. I appreciate that so much. Now, _____, you're next. Let's hear from you!" This type of group leadership is often needed when women are involved in good, fun fellowship. And even sometimes during the Bible study discussions. You may ask if one of the Heart Moms you work with has some experience with this type of monitoring and she may be responsible for this job.

Bible Study Lesson

The Bible study lesson is the meat of the evening, where Moms and Sisters dig into the Scriptures and matters of faith. Lessons come together better when prepared in advance. If there is more than one Heart Group, it's really nice when all groups are doing the same lessons. Of course Heart Moms can adapt the lesson to their own teaching styles and are encouraged to be creative. For example, one may plan the lesson around a craft while another does a different activity.

Care needs to be taken, though, that the heart of the lesson isn't lost in the fun and games. My experience with many, many young women is they cherish and look forward to digging deeper into the challenges the Bible asks of our lives. So don't shy away from rich, meaningful Bible study and challenging questions that require personal application of Scripture.

And it is important to facilitate personal sharing among the women. Different lessons will speak to and prompt revelations and thoughts and comments from different Sisters. This can be a very special time of seeking guidance from Scripture and gaining encouragement and support from the young Sisters and the older Moms. As they leave the Bible study, the young women should feel that their spirits have been given a boost and they have truly connected with each other in the group as they went through the lesson from the Lord together.

Heart Mom Moment

At the end of each Bible study, Heart Moms hand out some advice or instruction as a Heart Mom moment. This is designed to encourage Heart Sisters during the time between meetings. It is also designed as a reminder of what they've learned during the evening and how they need to intentionally implement the lesson in their daily lives. This is a way to put the Bible lesson and the focus of the evening into a practical application.

As the Moms get to know their Sisters better, they will have their own ideas of what to assign or what type of handout to send them off with. Here are a few examples:

- One night a week have a special dinner. Set the table with your best dishes and linens. Get flowers. Turn off the TV. Treat your family (or yourself, if single) to a delicious meal. Relax and enjoy each other's company as you pamper yourself in your own home.

- Begin each day with prayer for your family members. Get up a few minutes earlier than usual or use part of your morning schedule (such as praying while you brush your teeth or while cooking breakfast). Be specific in bringing each name before the Father. Later in the day, tell each family member in words or via a note that you've prayed for him or her that day. Pay attention to any difference in the way you think, act, or feel toward them.

- Take your child to a nursing home or to visit an elderly shut-in. Or take a gift to a new mother. Or plan a way for your child to spend part of his or her allowance on a good cause. Talk to your kids about the godly service of helping those who are in need. Teach your children to serve others by example and by letting them help you serve.

Take-Home Gift or Favor

Heart Group meetings are each specially planned, and they create wonderful moments and memories for the younger women. Sending the Sisters home with a special memento will help them remember the evening even more. It's also just one last reminder that the Moms are thinking about them.

Heart Moms can take turns purchasing or making something for each Sister to take home. (Important: do not break the budget on these. Homemade cookies are an example of something personal and special but inexpensive.) Some suggested favors are:

- Homemade fridge magnets with the evening's Scripture verse
- Baked goodies
- Handmade crafts such as candles, holiday decorations, sachets, cards (these can add to the evening's fun if created during the meeting)
- Trinkets—things like coffee mugs, candle holders, or seasonal home accessories purchased from a budget or dollar store that reflect the evening's theme
- Printed copies of parts of the Bible lesson or scriptures used

I've noticed that Heart Sisters look forward to seeing what "little something" they'll get at the end of the night. But, Moms, do not spend a lot on the gifts. There are many websites that offer ideas for making or purchasing things that will communicate care without breaking the bank.

A Word about the Menfolk

Heart Moms find that a great deal of their time is spent on their Sisters and on creating a meaningful experience for the younger women. This can disrupt the home life—especially when a group of happy, hungry ladies descends upon the house. Each Heart Mom should take the time to discuss plans with her husband and be considerate of his feelings. Make sure the meeting date and time work for him (imagine if he'd planned a romantic dinner out that night because he didn't know you'd be busy). Encourage his support, but certainly do not expect him to participate, except possibly by praying for your work in the ministry. I have learned that most men respond to their need for relationships by doing things differently than women would. Some men might enjoy small group activities. But for most, it's unlikely they would choose to host a dinner or plan a small group fellowship with other men. They would perhaps instead invite someone to go hunting or attend a sports event in order to get to know him better.

But who knows, your husband may enjoy showing hospitality so much he starts to help you—like with the cleanup. I have known quite a few husbands, including mine, who are happy their wives are involved in a Titus 2 ministry. It sure is nice when they are. So, again, if you are married, I encourage you to talk to your husband and ask him to be praying for your work as a mentor. In this way, his spiritual support will take on even more importance to both of you.

It's also encouraged that each Heart Sister prearrange this night with her husband. It's always better to give him a heads-up rather than mention you'll be gone for several hours as you head out the door! Getting your husband involved from the get-go with the plans for the children for the evening is always a great idea also. If a hubby has a church softball game or a late work meeting, Sisters can know early enough to make other arrangements for their children.

One important note: if your husband objects to your involvement or to hosting a Heart Group, then perhaps the timing is not right. In such a case, ask him to pray for this ministry and for the right way and time for you to be involved. Perhaps another year would be better for the both of you.

Do What's Best

Heart to Home groups have been successfully building relationships, sharing hospitality, studying God's Word, and bridging the generations for more than ten years. Our program is in churches all over the country and is going strong in these places. The program is well established and, most important, has seen God's blessings on it at every step of the way. Each year the program builds on the success of the past year.

I want you to know why I believe this is so. Heart to Home has its basis in the Word of God. As we have seen throughout this book, Titus 2:3–5 is a valuable biblical teaching for women to pay attention to. There are few Bible verses or commands given directly to women in God's Word. This is one of them.

And I believe Heart to Home is in direct obedience to this teaching. That is why Heart to Home's program has been successful. It has nothing to do with the people who have planned it or work in it, no matter how hard. I truly believe Heart to Home blesses many because we are just doing His work. I believe it has everything to do with God's faithfulness to bless us when we follow His instructions. We are simply doing what He tells us to do.

While Heart to Home is a successful mentoring program, promoting this specific ministry is not my goal. These ideas and plans have been tested in thousands of meetings, but in the end they are only suggestions. The overarching goal of the program—and this book—is to foster intergenerational fellowship and faith growth based on the teachings of Titus 2. I truly believe we are to be in close relationship with women in our churches in order to fulfill God's plan and purpose for us as His people.

Whatever you decide to do about a mentoring relationship or program, have fun with your Titus 2–based ministry and foster those relationships between the older and younger generations. Be sure you provide ways for women to share practical knowledge and godly wisdom, provide encouragement, and encourage prayer. See to needs and promote praise! And everything in between. Create friendships and a support system that will last for years to come.

I've said it before and I'll say it again: I know each of you involved in creating or participating in a Titus 2–based women's mentoring ministry will be transformed in ways you can't even imagine. I will be praying for you as you begin your adventure.

A Note to Heart Moms and Mentors

Heart Moms have a very precious task. The lives of multiple young women are entrusted to their care. So I encourage you to pray—and pray some more—about your decision to become a Heart Mom. Ask yourself if you have the time and the passion to mentor the younger generation. If you don't feel you have the time, energy, or resources to put into it right now, there is no shame in saying so. It's better to clarify that upfront than to affect your Heart Sisters' experience because you can't give them the attention they need.

Keep in mind that successful groups have more than one Heart Mom. This is intentional not only because each mature woman brings a different skill set to the table but also because they can share the tasks involved. This may help you as you make your decision. Your responsibilities of mentoring are shared. This is a great opportunity for you to work with your friends in a terrific ministry.

You may question whether or not you have what it takes to be a Heart Mom. I want to reassure you: there is no specific, perfect model of a Heart Mom. We are all different. We all make mistakes. We all have good and bad days. We all have struggles.

But we continue to show up. We're there for our young Christian sisters. We show them our true selves, warts and all, demonstrate our intentional love for them, and trust that God is in the details. Part of our job as mentors is to show younger women the faithfulness of God to be there for us during our crises, struggles, faults, and mistakes.

If you have had life experiences, if you love God and know He has worked in your family, and if you believe He can and will do the same in the lives of the Heart Sisters, then you're able to be a Heart Mom. It's that simple. Yes, there are things to learn, but the main requirement is to be a willing and loving servant of God. The rest will come.

Some things to consider as you ponder your choices:

- A Heart Mom is not perfect.
- A Heart Mom doesn't necessarily have formal training.
- A Heart Mom may be a woman who has made it through the many challenges of marriage and/or mothering.
- A Heart Mom may be a single woman who has never married or a widow or divorced woman who has experienced God's faithfulness.
- A Heart Mom is eager to share her experiences.
- A Heart Mom has learned and is still learning from mistakes and successes.
- A Heart Mom is willing to share the insights she's gained.
- A Heart Mom has experienced God's guiding hand in her life.
- A Heart Mom is wise and discerning and encouraging.

If you feel the above qualities reflect your heart and your passion, and you want to take that step and agree to be a Heart Mom, then . . . welcome! You are going to have an amazing adventure. A fulfilling time. How can you not? You will be guiding precious women toward a closer relationship with you, with each other, and with God. And I promise you will find the experience is just as much about you as it is about them. It will change you in ways you never dreamed.

Mentoring is not always easy, but it should always be intentional. I encourage you to take time to foster relationships with each of your Sisters. Share your life with them through your friendship. These young ladies are your spiritual children for a season. You are their spiritual mom. So the responsibility falls to you to make them feel as though they are treasured by you. Some ideas for letting them know how you care include:

- Call them up to invite them out for coffee or to share a meaningful scripture.
- Arrange a play day with a young mom and her children or offer to babysit for a date night.
- Have a young couple over for dinner or take them out.
- Send e-mails, cards, or notes to the Sisters in your group to remind them you're thinking about them.
- Encourage the talents or gifts you see in the Sisters.

There are countless ways you can show your Heart Sisters how much they mean to you. Keep in mind that when you do something for them, you are modeling behaviors they will in turn learn to show to the people they love.

My friend, I thank you for your willingness to be a part of a Titus 2–based ministry, whether it's Heart to Home or another. Without your and other mentors' commitments, this program could not exist. I want to encourage you with this: young women are eager to be in a close relationship with older women. God planted this desire deep within us. I can promise, based on my efforts and time in this ministry, that you will be richly blessed as you open your heart and your home to the young women in your church and community.

I pray that the young women who will be in your care as you mentor them will know the richness and depth of God's love, grace, and mercy through you. And most of all, I pray it will have the blessing of eternal importance for everyone involved.

God bless you.

Acknowledgments

First, my gratitude to my main editor, Jeana Ledbetter. Worthy has a worthy woman in you. I know they know that. But I'm just saying it. And, Jennifer Stair, you have been such an encourager. You are a lovely lady in spirit and deed. Thanks to all the design, marketing, sales, and super-smart people at Worthy who got behind this effort and made it all happen.

Buckets of thank-yous to my precious friend Leslie, for building the skeleton of this book and then with supreme patience (with me) outfitting it with the heart, the flesh, and the blood it needed. I am not exaggerating when I say this book never would have happened without you. I am beyond grateful to you and for you. Most of all, I know I have been blessed that God put us together on this project. You are a dear sister in Christ. My true, real, and authentic Jesus friend.

Thank you, Johnny. Truly a miracle worker for me. You move mountains. Wow!

I have been blessed with several forever friends. How could I even do life without Lauren? You have been my rock. Without you in my life, Heart to Home would not even function. I am so grateful for your love for me and for our common ministry. Stephanie, I can't even write your name without tearing up thinking of you and all you have meant to me. For years, you and I were the pioneers—dreaming and scheming, praying and putting into words, pictures, and action all that God continuously put on our hearts. You made so much of it happen with me and for me. Thank you from the bottom of my heart. Mindy, your life is a story—and certainly not a fairy tale. Your generosity in sharing your pain, struggles, and triumphs through it all constantly inspires me. Your faith in your heavenly Father is at a depth I hope to feel one day. Maranda, how you have blessed me, girlfriend! Thank you for being who you are and allowing God to use you from the beginning to mold you. I have watched you become putty in His hands. My blessings—my friends: I am not worthy of any of your friendships. But I am honored and grateful for each of you. My forever friends, we'll be in eternity together and get to rock on the porch of heaven, sweet teas in hand, as long as we want!

Missy Robertson and Kay Robertson are two of the most inspiring, biblically sound, courageous, and honorable friends I have ever been blessed to have. Your faith in me and in Heart to Home strengthens the foundations of the Heart to Home ministry constantly. You fuel the fire in me for women's ministry through your devotion to Heart to Home in word and deed. Thank you for all you have done to make all of this possible. I offer you my prayers for God's blessings over you as my meager thank-you. And I humbly seek His favor on you and your families forever.

My mom and mother-in-love are my greatest cheerleaders. Their uncompromising, biased support for me builds me up regularly. So much of what I believe and do for Jesus is because of these two strong, godly women. Thank You, God, for giving me these two examples of unselfish devotion to faith in Jesus and to our family.

I am privileged to get to love on and be loved by two women who are the closest friends I have on earth. My daughter, Katelyn, and my daughter-in-love, Jamie. You two shape my days with your (and my) intense love for your children and your husbands. You inspire my ministry and me! God bless you in all the busyness of your hands and your homes. And may His heart continue to shine through you. You are the dearest people on earth to me (along with your boys and husbands, of course). My big boys—Josh, Jake, and Grant—you are fine men of God. Keep loving Him and your charges. I am so proud of you and love you so much. To my grandboys: Honey's heart overflows. I love you to the moon and back.

Praise God, most of all, for the most amazing husband and friend on the planet. God never has replicated you. You are one of a kind, Randy. To put up with my erratic schedules, early-morning focus days, late nights, not to mention the normal moodiness and crazy requests that go along with being married to me, your patience is boundless. I am the most blessed woman ever to have walked the earth. Thank you for allowing my life in the Lord's kingdom work to press on and to matter. Without your moment-by-moment support, none of it would have ever happened. You have filled my tank, my love bank, my dreams, my needs, my wants, and my hopes over and over and over again. Forever love! God, please give us years more of a loving lifetime to be with our grands and kids.

A New Story—
Heartfelt Ministries

Now, my friend, I'm excited to invite you to celebrate with us as the next phase is developing for our rapidly expanding ministry. The plans God has prepared for us are exploding as this book goes to print.

Since 2003, we have been privileged to share our Titus 2 mentoring ministry with thousands of women as Heart to Home. We have prayed and planned, laughed and cried with our ministry leaders over the years since Heart to Home launched. We have asked God to lead us to open doors, hearts, and homes in ways that will bless and honor Him.

I am full of joy and gratitude that the work we have done as Heart to Home will continue as Heartfelt Ministries in 2015. This name change is a beautiful example of how God works in the details of our lives. The Bible tells us that when God decides to do something new, He often announces a name change. For example, Abram became Abraham, Jacob's name was changed to Israel, and Saul was renamed Paul as God intensified His work in their lives. This same name change has shown up in our ministry as Heart to Home becomes Heartfelt Ministries. I am thrilled and amazed at God's blessing on our hearts and hands.

About the Author

Dr. Joneal Kirby is founding director of Heart to Home Ministry, a women's mentoring program and conference based on Titus 2:3–5. She is the author of *Heart of a Family for Mom: Common Sense Parenting with Wisdom from the Word* and *Hope for YOUR Family: Six Keys to Connecting with Your Teen,* in addition to more than fifty Bible studies.

Dr. Kirby earned a PhD in marriage and family therapy from the University of Louisiana–Monroe. After years as a teacher and a school guidance counselor, she founded the Christian Counseling and Resource Center in West Monroe, Louisiana. She hosted the Legacy Network's talk show *Girlfriends,* hosts the daily *Heart to Home Radio* show, and is a regular contributor to magazines and newspapers on family issues. She and her husband host an annual marriage retreat and have taught marriage and parenting classes together for thirty years. Dr. Kirby speaks at conferences nation-wide with a unique speaking style that combines practical advice and humor with biblical wisdom and is rooted in her passion for strengthening families.

Dr. Kirby and her husband, Randy, are graduates of Harding University. The Kirbys have been married since July 12, 1975. They are members at White's Ferry Road Church of Christ in West Monroe, Louisiana, where Randy serves as an elder and Joneal as the women's ministry leader. They have three children, a daughter-in-love and a son-in-love, and four grandsons.

WORTHY®
PUBLISHING

If you enjoyed this book, will you consider sharing the message with others?

- Mention the book in a Facebook post, Twitter update, Pinterest pin, blog post, or upload a picture through Instagram.

- Recommend this book to those in your small group, book club, workplace, and classes.

- Head over to facebook.com/worthypublishing, "LIKE" the page, and post a comment as to what you enjoyed the most.

- Tweet "I recommend reading #Heartfelt by @theheartmom // @worthypub"

- Pick up a copy for someone you know who would be challenged and encouraged by this message.

- Write a book review online.

You can subscribe to Worthy Publishing's newsletter at worthypublishing.com.

WORTHY PUBLISHING
FACEBOOK PAGE

WORTHY PUBLISHING
WEBSITE